PLAN TO TURN YOUR COMPANY AROUND IN 90 DAYS

HOW TO RESTORE POSITIVE CASH FLOW AND PROFITABILITY

Jonathan H. Lack

Apress

Plan to Turn Your Company Around in 90 Days: How to Restore Positive Cash Flow and Profitability

ISBN-13 (pbk): 978-1-4302-4668-8

ISBN-13 (electronic): 978-1-4302-4669-5

Distributed to the book trade worldwide by Springer Science+Business Media New York, 233 Spring Street, 6th Floor, New York, NY 10013. Phone 1-800-SPRINGER, fax (201) 348-4505, e-mail orders-ny@springer-sbm.com, or visit www.springeronline.com. Apress Media, LLC is a California LLC and the sole member (owner) is Springer Science + Business Media Finance Inc (SSBM Finance Inc). SSBM Finance Inc is a Delaware corporation.

For information on translations, please e-mail rights@apress.com, or visit www.apress.com.

Apress and friends of ED books may be purchased in bulk for academic, corporate, or promotional use. eBook versions and licenses are also available for most titles. For more information, reference our Special Bulk Sales–eBook Licensing web page at www.apress.com/bulk-sales.

Any source code or other supplementary materials referenced by the author in this text is available to readers at www.apress.com. For detailed information about how to locate your book's source code, go to www.apress.com/source-code/.

Apress Business: The Unbiased Source of Business Information

Apress business books provide essential information and practical advice, each written for practitioners by recognized experts. Busy managers and professionals in all areas of the business world—and at all levels of technical sophistication—look to our books for the actionable ideas and tools they need to solve problems, update and enhance their professional skills, make their work lives easier, and capitalize on opportunity.

Whatever the topic on the business spectrum—entrepreneurship, finance, sales, marketing, management, regulation, information technology, among others—Apress has been praised for providing the objective information and unbiased advice you need to excel in your daily work life. Our authors have no axes to grind; they understand they have one job only—to deliver up-to-date, accurate information simply, concisely, and with deep insight that addresses the real needs of our readers.

It is increasingly hard to find information—whether in the news media, on the Internet, and now all too often in books—that is even-handed and has your best interests at heart. We therefore hope that you enjoy this book, which has been carefully crafted to meet our standards of quality and unbiased coverage.

We are always interested in your feedback or ideas for new titles. Perhaps you'd even like to write a book yourself. Whatever the case, reach out to us at `editorial@apress.com` and an editor will respond swiftly. Incidentally, at the back of this book, you will find a list of useful related titles. Please visit us at `www.apress.com` to sign up for newsletters and discounts on future purchases.

The Apress Business Team

This book is dedicated to the entrepreneurs and small business owners across America who are not only the backbone of our economy, but also a big inspiration for the American way of life.

Contents

About the Author

Jonathan H. Lack is principal of ROI Ventures, LLC, which specializes in strategic planning and company turnarounds. He has more than 20 years of experience in operations management and strategic planning, focusing primarily on consumer product, manufacturing, and services companies. He has experience across all company sizes—startups, midsize, and *Fortune* 500—and in a number of industries, including financial services, food and beverage, information services, health care, financial/Internet, manufacturing, and telecom. Lack served as Director of Alternative Investments for Galapagos Partners, LP, a MultiFamily Office in which he currently advises on special projects. He was part of the founding executive management of CompuBank, NA, the first Internet bank to receive a charter from the U.S. Treasury Office of the Comptroller of the Currency (OCC). Lack led the bank to achieving one of the industry's fastest growth rates, and he developed brand recognition and customer confidence that earned it the #1 Online Bank ranking by Smart Money magazine. Lack has helped raise more than $36 million in angel, institutional, corporate, and private-equity funding in four separate deals. He holds an MBA from Wharton, an MA from John Hopkins University School of Advanced International Studies (SAIS), and a BA in Middle East Studies from the University of California.

Acknowledgments

I want to thank a number of people for whom this book would not be possible, starting with Apress's Jeff Olson, who encouraged me to write the book, and Rita Fernando and her team of editors who did a fantastic job of cleaning up my grammar and pushing me to clarify my thoughts. A special note of appreciation goes out to my former SAIS classmate, consulting partner, and good friend Keith Bickel, PhD, who was my sounding board on a biweekly basis throughout the past year. I thank my Wharton buddies Charles Boyd, Wael Salam, and Michael Varner, and my CompuBank colleagues and friends Bill Krull and Terry Puster, who have been great confidants and supporters in good times and bad throughout my business career and personal life. A special thanks goes to my brother Stephen Lack, who has not only been a great sibling, but also a good friend, client, and mentor. In addition, I thank my sister Sharon Stein, brother-in-law Ross Stein, and consultant Nicholas Martinez for their support in helping me get to the finish line and complete this book. Last, I thank my son Noah for his support during this past year and for allowing me to work on the book during his many basketball practices.

Introduction

Reversing Business Insanity

Your company is in trouble—or soon will be. Sales may be decreasing, it's getting harder and harder to eke out a profit, and you may suspect you've already started the death spiral that causes so many companies to crash and burn.

Based on my experience as an entrepreneur, as a consultant advising companies about strategic planning, and as an interim chief executive officer (CEO) when a rapid turnaround is required, I suspect that you and your fellow executives are committed to achieving the firm's vision and mission but are extremely frustrated, unsure of what to do, and may be burned out. Employee morale is probably dipping along with the company's sales. In addition, the firms' debt and payables are most likely increasing. No matter how unique your product or service, this trend is choking your firm's chance of success and is simply unsustainable.

If you are old enough to be reading this book, you probably have read and/or heard that one definition of insanity is doing the same thing over and over again and expecting different results. Many of us have not only heard this definition, but have been susceptible to it in our personal lives as well as in business. I suspect that the reason you are reading this book is because your company is suffering from business insanity. This book is intended to help your firm by doing what a good friend once advised me: *If you want to climb out of a hole, stop digging.*

As counterintuitive as it may seem—and as difficult as it may be for you to hear—the company culture must change very quickly for your firm to survive. What worked in the past is simply not working today and certainly will not be effective tomorrow. Chances are that your firm's culture has been product or service oriented, personality driven, and impulsive—characteristics viewed by all, proudly, as creative—which may have worked during the startup and growth phases, but must now change. The faster the firm becomes customer centric, process oriented, and metric centric, the faster it will start to reverse the negative trends it is experiencing.

Chances are that you and your managers do not need to work any harder, you need to work smarter. The first step in doing this is to conduct an objective assessment of what is working and what is not. The firm did not get into its current predicament overnight, and it is not going to get out of it overnight, either. However, within 90 days or less, you can develop a plan to turn your company around by evaluating every aspect of your business using the tools and principles discussed in following chapters.

Here's what not to do: panic or conduct wholesale firings, like so many private equity firms and venture capitalists do when faced with turning around a struggling company. Firing the CEO and senior managers may feel good, but often it is not the most effective approach to solving your problems. Even if it is, new managers still need to conduct an extensive audit so they do not become vulnerable to reinventing the wheel and/or making the same mistakes as previous management. Besides, if you are a CEO or part of senior management or owner of a family business, cleaning house of executive management is not a viable option. Are you going to fire yourself?

This book is intended to help owners, managers, accountants, bankers, consultants, entrepreneurs, investors, and lawyers help get a company back on track as quickly and cost-effectively as possible. And this can and does happen. Since earning my MBA from The Wharton School more than 20 years ago, I have been involved directly with a number of startups and dozens of companies that were facing the very problems I review in this book. Most of the issues I cover were not learned at Wharton; rather, I learned them from the School of Hard Knocks. I have found myself in many of the situations discussed in this book. At the time, I was not aware of outside resources that could have helped me find solutions faster. This book provides a no-nonsense, straightforward approach to solving everyday business problems for a company that, for whatever reason, has lost its momentum and finds itself digging out of a deep hole.

Road Map of the Book

Plan to Turn Your Company Around in 90 Days is divided into four parts. There is a logical sequence to the parts and their chapters. However, each part and each chapter can stand on its own merit and thus does not need to be read in sequence for you to gain valuable insights.

Part I focuses on managing and preserving cash flow. This is the most important section for any CEO and/or senior-level manager to understand. If you don't understand everything in this section, read it a second time. If you need to, discuss the issues with a more financially oriented advisor or friend. Having a better grasp of cash flow management is critical to turning your company around. It will also help you understand the context of the subsequent parts and chapters.

Part I is comprised of three chapters. Chapter 1, How to Manage Cash Flow Better, focuses on why managing cash flow should be the number one priority of the firm. Chapter 2, How to Manage Accounts Payables Better, focuses on tips to manage your accounts payable. Chapter 3, How to Manage Accounts Receivables Better, focuses on tips for managing accounts receivables.

Part II examines improving operations management. It is critical that you determine where, in the firm, you are getting value for your expenditures and where you are wasting money. Your management team is going to have to develop a discipline of understanding which expenditures are necessary to run your business, as opposed to the nice-to-haves, during the initial phases of turning the company around. The latter point is especially important given your limited working capital.

Part II, Improving Operations Management, is comprised of three chapters. Chapter 4, How to Manage Employee Productivity Better, focuses on managing employee productivity by, among other things, improving internal communications. Chapter 5, How to Manage Technology, Facilities, and Manufacturing Better, examines leveraging the assets you need and reducing the liabilities associated with them, as well as getting rid of what your firm does not need. Chapter 6, How to Manage Process Flows Better, looks at how to manage your core business operations more effectively to maximize your overall productivity and margins.

Part III is called Increasing Marketing and Sales Efficiency, which is the one area of the business in which it is very easy to become susceptible to third-party marketers and advertisers who get paid to sell you programs and who often have no clue and, sometimes, no interest in whether you really need their services. Marketing and sales is especially difficult for consumer-oriented businesses that are dependent on customers who have lots of other choices for purchasing the same products and services, as well as other unrelated companies vying for the same precious, disposable wallet share given the current lingering recession.

Part III is comprised of comprised of three chapters. Chapter 7, How to Understand Your Customers, Competitors, and Key Trends Better, looks at how understanding your clients, competitors, and industry trends will enable your firm to position itself more effectively in the marketplace. Chapter 8, How to Develop a More Effective Marketing Strategy, examines why developing a solid marketing plan should occur before developing a sales plan. Chapter 9, How to Develop a More Effective Sales Strategy, focuses on developing a sales strategy along with a motivated, trained, and accountable sales team.

Part IV, Managing from the Top Down, explores how to manage your investors and the board of directors, yourself and your staff, and an outside consultant. This is an area in which CEOs in trouble tend to put the least amount of effort. The main emphasis in this part is on the importance of transparency and maintaining ongoing communication with those stakeholders who ultimately may be your greatest asset in turning around your firm.

Part IV is comprised of three chapters. Chapter 10, How to Manage Investors and the Board of Directors Better, looks at how to reach out to your investors and board members, and the importance of leveraging their relevant expertise and contacts to help your company. Chapter 11, How to Hire and Manage Your Turnaround Consultant, examines the processes of finding, engaging, and managing a consultant to help you turn your company around. Chapter 12, How to Manage Yourself and Your Staff Better, focuses on helping you do some things for yourself and your staff that might make all of you more effective.

Turnarounds: Simple, But Not Easy

Every company's financial and operational situation, culture, and dynamics are different. However, the fundamentals of operating any business and the problems to which many companies are vulnerable are not that unique. This entire book is based on firsthand experience of helping different types of companies work through very similar problems.

First, you need to get your finances in order. This does not mean you have to solve all your financial problems; it means you have to understand how big your problem is and where and why you are losing money. Second, you need to get your operations in order. Third, you need to improve your marketing and sales. Understanding which products and/or services sell the best to whom, and which ones make the best margins is critical before planning marketing and sales efforts. Fourth, and last, you need to manage yourself, your fellow executives and staff, your board, your investors, and your consultants better. This old cliché is trite but true: the most valuable resource your firm has is people. Spending the appropriate time building your team and leveraging its strengths is critical to getting your company back on track. Together, these steps will allow you to make your way out of your hole.

Plan to Turn Your Company Around in 90 Days is intended to be a lifeline for you and your colleagues. I hope that many of the recommendations made throughout the following chapters help get your company back on track as soon as possible. Feel free to e-mail me with any questions (jlack@roi.com). Good luck!

PART

I

Managing and Preserving Cash Flow

CHAPTER

1

How to Manage Cash Flow Better

Your Number One Priority

It's important to point out at the onset of this book that you shouldn't worry about your firm's original vision or how big your company is going to get someday. Your business is in survival mode. Preserving cash must be your top priority, along with fixing the systemic problems that your company faces.

In addition, you should focus on how to make your business profitable. As a result, your company may have to downsize its staff, locations, operations, and marketing campaigns to obtain gross profitability. Simply selling more products or services that are not profitable only leads to the faster demise of your firm. If you can't obtain gross profitability, you have a flawed business model that needs dissecting as quickly as possible. If you do have a profitable business model but are unable to reach the company's full potential, there are various options available to you to get the firm back on track. We discuss these choices throughout this book.

If people try to convince you that all you need to do is just grow your way out of the hole the firm is in, chances are they are either not aware of the systemic problems your business is facing or they have never been involved with a company that has the same types of problems you have. It takes working capital to grow a business, whether you are hiring new sales representatives, purchasing advertising, or purchasing inventory. If you are out of cash, you simply cannot do these things. You must play a different hand as quickly as possible; you don't have any more time to waste.

The Importance of Cash Flow

It is worth repeating that if your firm is running out of cash quickly and has a long list of payables as well as receivables, managing your company's cash flow must be your number one priority, although this is not to say that there are not other critical problems the business is facing that must be addressed, improved, and better managed moving forward. The next actions you take may have a short-term negative impact on some aspects of your business, such as sales and employee morale. However, regardless of how counterintuitive it may be to you or members of your management team, the priorities you set to move the company forward should point toward improving cash flow.

Cash buys you the time you need to fix the other problems the company must address. This doesn't mean that throwing money at every problem in your company solves a problem. In some cases, having access to too much credit and capital only exacerbates a systemic issue that must be dealt with in a more prudent manner.

If you run out of cash after tapping out your line of credit and if your vendors are calling for overdue payments and are no longer willing to provide you with critical materials and supplies to run your business, the game is over. You could try to restructure your firm's debt through bankruptcy. However, this is a strategy you should discuss with a bankruptcy attorney. Bankruptcy is not discussed in this book. There is no guarantee that, once you go down the bankruptcy path, your current management will be able to remain involved with the company.

Even if you plan to raise another round of capital, your savvy investors are going to insist you have a plan to get the company on track so that, at a minimum, they are confident they are going to get their money back—plus a return—for risking more of their capital. This book gives you a framework and tools to develop a strategic plan to put your company back on track.

Getting Started

The first step in managing your firm's cash flow is to develop a clear understanding of where the cash is going. You must track every penny that goes out the door and then determine how you can either get a better return on that investment of funds or reduce and stop that expenditure immediately. Regardless of how well you think you know the company's cash outflow, there is no substitute for having an accurate report. The report must reflect your monthly and yearly cash outflow, broken down into discretionary costs, discretionary fixed costs, and fixed costs.

Figure 1-1 is an example of one such report. I recommend you start with the current month in the first column and add the remaining months of the year across the top of each column, going out 12 months. The first row under the header contains the cash balance at the beginning of the month. The next row contains your expected cash from sales. (Cash flow does not include your receivables—only the actual cash received.) The next row contains aged receivables. I separate this row from current sales because most of the expenses associated with these aged receivables should have already been spent, unless they are listed in the aged payables category, which I put in the debt section at the bottom of the example. The next row, Total Cash Inflow, should be the total of the two previous rows just discussed. The next row, Total Disbursements for Month, should be a total of all the expenses listed in the sales and marketing, payroll, operations, and debt section of the budget. The end-of-the-month cash balance is the balance of the total cash inflow less the total disbursements for the month.

If your end-of-month cash balance is negative, you need to cut your expenses as soon as possible before you run out of credit. Start by reviewing all your discretionary, discretionary fixed, fixed, as well as variable expenses.

Discretionary costs are those you have may have budgeted for or are a one-off opportunity for which you are not obligated to spend money. Discretionary fixed costs consist of expenditures you have budgeted for and have been paying every month, but have the option to reduce and even halt temporarily unilaterally. Fixed costs consist of what you are obligated contractually to pay monthly that you cannot cut unilaterally without renegotiating with your vendors and creditors, and without risking serious legal repercussions. Variable expenses are expenses tied to revenue (such as inventory, sales tax, hourly labor, and so forth).

Category	Month	Jan-13	Feb-13	Mar-13	Apr-13	May-13	Jun-13	Jul-13	Aug-13	Sep-13	Oct-13	Nov-13	Dec-13	Total
	Beginning of Month Cash Balance	-	-	-	-	-	-	-	-	-	-	-	-	-
	2013 Sales Received	-	-	-	-	-	-	-	-	-	-	-	-	-
	2012 Receivables Received	-	-	-	-	-	-	-	-	-	-	-	-	-
	Total Cash Inflow	-	-	-	-	-	-	-	-	-	-	-	-	-
	Total Disbursements for Month	-	-	-	-	-	-	-	-	-	-	-	-	-
	End of Month Cash Balance	-	-	-	-	-	-	-	-	-	-	-	-	-
	Sales & Marketing													
Discretionary	Advertising	-	-	-	-	-	-	-	-	-	-	-	-	-
Discretionary	Business Development	-	-	-	-	-	-	-	-	-	-	-	-	-
Discretionary	Conferences	-	-	-	-	-	-	-	-	-	-	-	-	-
Discretionary Fixed	Marketing Consultant	-	-	-	-	-	-	-	-	-	-	-	-	-
Discretionary	Trade Shows	-	-	-	-	-	-	-	-	-	-	-	-	-
Discretionary	Travel & Lodging	-	-	-	-	-	-	-	-	-	-	-	-	-
	Payroll (Salaried Staff)													
Discretionary Fixed	CEO	-	-	-	-	-	-	-	-	-	-	-	-	-
Discretionary Fixed	CFO	-	-	-	-	-	-	-	-	-	-	-	-	-
Discretionary Fixed	COO	-	-	-	-	-	-	-	-	-	-	-	-	-
Discretionary Fixed	Sales Manager	-	-	-	-	-	-	-	-	-	-	-	-	-
Discretionary Fixed	Support Staff 1	-	-	-	-	-	-	-	-	-	-	-	-	-
Discretionary Fixed	Support Staff 2	-	-	-	-	-	-	-	-	-	-	-	-	-
Discretionary Fixed	Support Staff 3	-	-	-	-	-	-	-	-	-	-	-	-	-
Discretionary Fixed	Support Staff 4	-	-	-	-	-	-	-	-	-	-	-	-	-
Discretionary Fixed	Support Staff 5	-	-	-	-	-	-	-	-	-	-	-	-	-
	Operations													
Discretionary Fixed	Accountant	-	-	-	-	-	-	-	-	-	-	-	-	-
Fixed	Building Maintenance	-	-	-	-	-	-	-	-	-	-	-	-	-
Fixed	Cable/Internet Service	-	-	-	-	-	-	-	-	-	-	-	-	-
Fixed	Car Insurance	-	-	-	-	-	-	-	-	-	-	-	-	-
Fixed	Cell Phone	-	-	-	-	-	-	-	-	-	-	-	-	-
Discretionary Fixed	Cleaning Services	-	-	-	-	-	-	-	-	-	-	-	-	-
Variable	Contract hourly labor	-	-	-	-	-	-	-	-	-	-	-	-	-
Fixed	Electricity	-	-	-	-	-	-	-	-	-	-	-	-	-
Fixed	General Liability Insurance	-	-	-	-	-	-	-	-	-	-	-	-	-
Variable	Inventory Purchases	-	-	-	-	-	-	-	-	-	-	-	-	-
Discretionary Fixed	IT Support	-	-	-	-	-	-	-	-	-	-	-	-	-
Fixed	Natural Gas	-	-	-	-	-	-	-	-	-	-	-	-	-
Fixed	Office/Store Alarm	-	-	-	-	-	-	-	-	-	-	-	-	-
Discretionary Fixed	Payroll Processing Service Fee	-	-	-	-	-	-	-	-	-	-	-	-	-
Variable	Payroll taxes	-	-	-	-	-	-	-	-	-	-	-	-	-
Variable	Project related office supplies	-	-	-	-	-	-	-	-	-	-	-	-	-
Variable	Project related travel	-	-	-	-	-	-	-	-	-	-	-	-	-
Fixed	Rent													
Variable	Sales Taxes	-	-	-	-	-	-	-	-	-	-	-	-	-
Discretionary Fixed	Trash Service	-	-	-	-	-	-	-	-	-	-	-	-	-
Fixed	Web Hosting	-	-	-	-	-	-	-	-	-	-	-	-	-
	Debt													
Fixed	Building Note	-	-	-	-	-	-	-	-	-	-	-	-	-
Fixed	Credit Cards	-	-	-	-	-	-	-	-	-	-	-	-	-
Fixed	Line of Credit	-	-	-	-	-	-	-	-	-	-	-	-	-
Fixed	Past Due Payables	-	-	-	-	-	-	-	-	-	-	-	-	-

Figure 1-1. A sample cash flow budget

Table 1-1 shows examples of each of these types of costs, which are also listed next to the various expenditures in the left column in Figure 1-1.

Table 1-1. Examples of Types of Costs

Types	Example
Discretionary	Advertising, conferences, meals, trade shows, travel
Discretionary Fixed	Payroll, professional service contracts, cell phones
Fixed	Rent, equipment leases, insurance, loan payments
Variable	Inventory, hourly labor, sales tax

Your next step is to develop a budget of outflows. The goal is to reduce your cash burn rate dramatically without shutting down the business. When I worked at MCI (my first job out of business school), the chief executive officer (CEO) at the time sent out a cost-savings memo in which he said that a dollar saved was equivalent to $10 in revenue. Put another way, a company with a 10% net profit margin needs to book $10 in revenue to earn $1. The lesson: Cutting costs can have a powerful effect on your finances. The economics are no less true for smaller firms, and perhaps may be even greater for firms that have smaller margins. This powerful, effective assessment should not be overlooked.

Table 1-2 illustrates how much of an impact cost cutting can be compared with increasing revenues. This is not to say increasing revenues is not important—of course it is—but only after you have cut costs and done everything you can to increase your margins.

Table 1-2. Why Cost Cutting Is as Valuable as Revenue Growth*

Cost Cutting	Revenue Equivalents
$1	$10
$100	$1,000
$1,000	$10,000
$10,000	$100,000
$100,000	$1,000,000

**Assumes a 10% net profit margin.*

Improving your margins takes a lot of discipline because it is, most likely, not how you've been running your business. Many readers are going to think I'm crazy. Why wouldn't you want your top priority to be to bring in more cash through sales? You should want an immediate increase in sales only if there is gross profit in this cash stream and only if you are confident you are going to get paid in a timely manner. However, if you do get paid for your sales, and you are using this cash for payroll only and not for paying for materials that you purchased on credit to create the product you sold (not to mention sales tax and so on), you are merely digging a deeper hole and not focusing on the key problems that got your firm into the mess it currently faces.

Furthermore, what is really powerful about the assessment displayed in Table 1-2 is that, with the right objectivity and commitment, you can make these cuts within a matter of days, if not hours, whereas increasing revenues takes much longer and is dependent on a lot more uncontrollable factors, such as effectiveness of sales and marketing efforts, the willingness of your customers to purchase your product or service, macroeconomic trends, and more.

Although it is a valid point to say that cost reduction is dependent on an accurate sales forecast, I assume that your sales are flat or decreasing. Therefore, until you make systemic changes to your products, services, sales, and marketing strategy, you must segment your cash outflow into what the firm absolutely *must* have to keep the operation running and what you would *like* to have to grow the business, independent of your current revenues.

Tip Keep your eyes focused on the must-haves—the things that will keep you in business long term. Be honest with yourself; a lot of things you might think are essential—such as that company-leased car—is really a nice-to-have item that is impeding your firm's ability to survive.

This latter point may not make much sense to you. However, if your customers are not paying you on time—or at all—your sales in the short term are only depleting your precious materials or inventory, and you have limited or no ability to purchase more in the short term.

If you are still not convinced of my suggestion and are still asking yourself why I'm not recommending that sales be your top priority, skip ahead to Chapter 3. There, I show you that having more sales does not always guarantee you more cash in the short term, especially if you have a lot of aging receivables. Furthermore, as mentioned, selling more unprofitable products or services for which you owe money is only leading to a faster demise of your company.

Discretionary Costs/Expenses

Until you have conducted a marketing audit, as outlined in Chapter 8, to determine which products and services are keepers, which ones can be improved, as well as which ones should be discontinued, I recommend that you put an immediate stop to almost all your marketing and business development expenditures, including advertising, conferences, tradeshows, and travel. These are medium- to long-term investments. Given your firm's cash flow needs, the company is simply not in a position to make these types of expenditures at this juncture.

Note Marketing and business development efforts aren't always essential expenditures—especially if you're losing money on the sales you now have.

This decision will be considered absolutely insane by your marketing and business development staff and consultants. However, as the saying goes: Doing the same thing over and over again and expecting a different result is one definition of insanity. Let's be honest. Your overall branding and marketing efforts are not working; otherwise, your firm wouldn't be in its current predicament. Furthermore, after you develop and execute a strategic plan, your marketing efforts will be more valuable and thus more cost-effective. By putting an immediate stop to almost all your marketing and business development expenditures, your firm has a much better chance of growing its revenues.

Discretionary Fixed Costs/Expenses

Let's now review your discretionary fixed costs, such as payroll, professional services, cell phones, and so forth. The biggest discretionary fixed cost for almost all companies is payroll. It is, in my opinion one, of the most inefficient expenditures for most companies (as is marketing, which I discuss in Chapter 8). Hence, it is also the biggest opportunity for most companies to improve their return on investment (ROI) on that allocation.

There are a number of ways in which to improve your ROI on payroll. One way is to measure payroll as a percentage of revenue, as well as revenue per employee, then compare these metrics with industry norms to determine whether your firm is underperforming or overperforming. You can get these norms by talking to industry experts and by looking at the financials of public companies in your business sector.

Many investors look at these metrics to determine whether payroll should be cut, which is a fast way to reduce recurring monthly expenditures. Even if these metrics are not readily available, boards of directors often look to payroll as a natural place for company-saving cuts. However, these cuts, if not warranted, may create even bigger problems for the remaining employees because of the simple fact that they may be overwhelmed, not qualified to pick up the additional workload placed on them, and worried about their own job security to the point of reduced productivity.

Before going into the ways in which to cut payroll, let me outline a few payroll policies that you should implement immediately. The first is that you should track how many hours each of your employees works on a weekly basis, and ask for a mandatory weekly report from all employees or their managers regarding what was accomplished that week, what were the key challenges, and what are primary items on which to focus the next week. These reports should be turned in by close of business on Friday so that senior management has the weekend to review and determine how to maximize payroll resources for the next week.

If your firm has hourly staff, put an immediate ban on overtime into place—with no exceptions. Chances are that you have part-time staff that would be happy get more hours. Although it is understandable that some hourly employees want and need to work as many hours as possible, your company simply cannot afford to pay 50% more than what is budgeted for a specific activity, especially during a period when your firm is losing money and has limited and/or depleting cash.

Tip First step with hourly workers: Ban all overtime.

While you're at it, reiterate how many hours salaried employees and managers are expected to work. It is important that every employee, including senior and executive management, pull his or her weight. Everyone's livelihood is dependent on them doing so. It is also critical that all employees work smart and have a positive impact in their respective roles. To make this happen, management must do a better, smarter job. Managers—now and in the future—should ensure that all employees have a copy of their job description and a clear understanding of their goals and objectives. If you don't have job descriptions, start writing them immediately.

Even after doing everything possible to increase your staff's productivity, including better training when necessary, there simply may not be a need for some of your employees, given your firm's current predicament. Laying off workers is never an easy thing to do, especially during a lingering recession with high unemployment, and it is not always an objective process, nor is it always the fault of the persons getting laid off. Some firms try to avoid forced payroll cuts by offering a severance for anybody who wants to leave the company voluntarily; other firms cut back everyone's compensation equally by the percentage they are trying to save and/or go to a shorter work week. Having been laid off as well as having had to make payroll cuts, I recommend developing a well-thought-out and objective strategy for how you determine which positions are to be eliminated and how those individuals to be laid off will be compensated, if at all. Regardless of how it is decided who gets laid off and when, how you communicate it to these individuals and to the rest of your staff is critical for maintaining employee morale and productivity. It is at this juncture where leadership is critical, and where I have seen executive management fail miserably. Executives often hide behind a human resource manager and/or subordinate managers.

To plan for a layoff, make sure you have a spreadsheet that lists every employee on the payroll, including executive management, a brief job description, his or her monthly compensation, his or her percentage of the overall payroll, and a simple performance rating: overperformer, average performer, or underperformer.

Table 1-3 is an example of one way to determine where your firm can make the difficult-but-necessary payroll cuts. After you look at payroll expenditures by a percentage of the total, it becomes a lot less difficult to make an assessment about someone's value to the company, given its current predicament. You'll find very quickly that, until your sales kick back in, your biggest payroll savings may be with management, given how much greater a percentage their payroll costs are compared with those of the other staff.

Table 1-3. Sample Chart Showing Salaries and Rating Employee Value

Title	Role	Rating	Annual Salary	Monthly Salary	% of Total Payroll
President/CEO	Oversees company's direction, investors and staff	Average - performer	$175,000	$14,583	13%
COO	Manages daily operations	Average - performer	$125,000	$10,417	10%
CFO	Manages company's finances	Average - performer	$125,000	$10,417	10%
VP Sales	Manage sales reps	Under-performer	$125,000	$10,417	10%
VP Product Development	Manages product development	Over-performer	$100,000	$8,333	8%
Comptroller	Manages bookkeeping	Average - performer	$75,000	$6,250	6%
Sales Rep 1	Sell to and manage company's clients	Average - performer	$75,000	$6,250	6%
Sales Rep 2	Sell to and manage company's clients	Average - performer	$75,000	$6,250	6%
Sales Rep 3	Sell to and manage company's clients	Average - performer	$75,000	$6,250	6%
Sales Rep 4	Sell to and manage company's clients	Average - performer	$75,000	$6,250	6%
Customer Service Manager	Manages customer services reps	Average - performer	$50,000	$4,167	4%
Customer Service Rep 1	Support customer inquiries	Under-performer	$30,000	$2,500	2%
Customer Service Rep 2	Support customer inquiries	Average - performer	$30,000	$2,500	2%
Customer Service Rep 3	Support customer inquiries	Average - performer	$30,000	$2,500	2%
Customer Service Rep 4	Support customer inquiries	Under-performer	$30,000	$2,500	2%
Customer Service Rep 5	Support customer inquiries	Average - performer	$30,000	$2,500	2%
Customer Service Rep 6	Support customer inquiries	Average - performer	$30,000	$2,500	2%
Executive Assistant	Assists executive management	Average - performer	$30,000	$2,500	2%
Receptionist	Answers inbound calls	Average - performer	$30,000	$2,500	2%
Total Salary			$1,315,000	$109,583	100%

If your overperforming employees are true superstars, it is important that executive management let them know how much they are appreciated to keep them from jumping ship. Executives often make promises of future compensation if the company get turned around. When this happens, it is important that those promises are honored. In the interim, giving employees a well-deserved day off as well as making sure they don't work on weekends can go a long way in demonstrating how much they are valued.

Without contradicting the previous recommendation, it important that you have an objective perception of your overperforming employees, as well as the performance of your other employees. This knowledge can be difficult to obtain, unless your overperformers are sales representatives and their performance can be measured quantitatively. Chances are that most of your overperformers are committed to the company and pick up the roles of other employees who have been laid off or who have resigned. However, their zeal for jumping in and helping does not mean that these staff members are the most efficient and cost-effective employees for the roles they assume. In many instances, they are the least efficient because they are spread too thin and aren't able to perform their core responsibilities at an optimal level.

In some instances, these overperforming employees—although committed to the mission and vision of the firm—have bad work habits that are detrimental to the firm's success and may lack some critical skill sets. They may be the highest paid employees, but are the least likely to be able to make the necessary changes required for the company to succeed.

Note I have seen examples of so-called superstars being the hardest working and highest paid employees, but not the best ROI. Many of these employees are carrying the load for their CEO because he or she is burned out or incompetent in certain areas of the business. To their credit, I have also seen these overperformers offer to take on more responsibility when a manager's role becomes vacant and there are no funds to replace him or her. However, their broad institutional knowledge becomes a liability because, in part, they have used it as job security. I don't fault these types of overperformers. However, my role is to help you save your company and to know where to look for ways to save precious resources.

Tip Your superstars, believe it or not, may be expendable. Take a good look at the ROI with high-performing employees. It may be that your average employees can handle the workload at a lesser cost.

The firm's average employees are most likely the bulk of your staff. These employees are probably running on autopilot and have not been supervised close enough while management focuses on putting out the fires of the day or week. There is a good chance that some of these employees are part-time employees with a second or third job. Their duties could be divided up among a couple of full-time employees who could be more productive with better coaching and supervision. The reverse could be a possibility as well; you could eliminate a full-time position and delegate the core responsibilities to a part-time person.

Underperforming employees fall into two groups. The first group consists of employees that, for whatever reason, are not helping the company. Maybe they are burned out, have an attitude problem, or have alcohol or drug dependencies. These employees, as well as their colleagues, know their current role is not working out, but they aren't in a hurry to find another job because they've been able to keep their job regardless of their work habits (in part because they haven't been supervised adequately). And in many cases, they have limited opportunities to work elsewhere for a variety of reasons, such as drug testing or their inability to get along with colleagues.

The second group of underperformers consists of committed employees who are floundering in their current role, in part, because they were set up unintentionally for failure. They may be required to achieve unrealistic goals without the necessary training, or without the operational, marketing, and management support to be successful at their job.

I recommend laying off the first group of underperformers as soon as possible. All layoffs must be done in accordance with your state employment laws. In some instances, employee morale may actually improve when this group of employees is no longer working at the firm. Some staff members will know these workers should have been let go long ago and will cheer their departure.

Next, although I'm in favor of removing an unnecessary and/or unfixable floundering position, I recommend that you do your best to find the second group of underperforming employees another role in the company. Chances are that, with better supervision, a strategy, and ongoing support, these employees can become a loyal, valuable part of your team. In some instances, however, given the company's survival mode, you may not be in a position to give this second group of employees another chance, and you may have to lay them off as well.

Tip Get rid of underperforming employees who are incapable of helping the company dig out of the hole it's in. Work with the employees who are underperforming through no fault of their own. Provide training or better supervision, restructure their jobs or move them into new ones, and do whatever it takes to help them (and your company) succeed.

Third-Party Professional Services

It is important that management also take a serious look at how it can cut back on retainer relationships the firm has with information technology (IT) contractors, marketing/public relations firms, cleaning services, cell phones companies, and so forth. As mentioned, it is absolutely critical that you make a distinction between what you think is nice to have versus absolute must-haves. This discernment process can be difficult for managers who worked hard to obtain and retain these relationships with third-party vendors, and they may feel their reputation is at stake when these relationships are severed. Nonetheless, it is important to leave egos at the door and to be as objective as possible. Every dollar saved is a dollar that was probably being wasted, and one the firm can't afford to lose.

I've seen companies retain marketing consultants or ad agencies that provided absolutely limited or no value to the client. I've taken heat from both my clients and their consultants or agencies because I strongly recommended halting marketing expenditures. In most cases, these third parties should be embarrassed by how ineffective their efforts are in affecting the company's top line. After I share the financial results of their efforts with them, they usually realize they need to find another client fast. This isn't to say they aren't talented, but they weren't, however, managed properly by the CEO and were more concerned with their own cash flow than that of their client.

Fixed Costs

There's nothing you can do about fixed costs, right? Wrong. Even if your firm has contractual fixed costs, it doesn't mean you shouldn't try to renegotiate the terms of these commitments.

Leases

The first step in evaluating fixed costs is to conduct an audit of all your locations to determine whether you need all of them. These locations include offices, storefronts, manufacturing facilities, and warehouses. You need to justify every expenditure.

The best way to start this exercise is to create a simple spreadsheet with recurring expenditures. What locations can you get rid of as quickly as possible? If you have a retail location that is losing money and not making any gross margin contribution to the business, for example, close down that location. If you have multiple storage units or warehouses that are not being used to their capacity, figure out how you can consolidate them. If you have empty office space, sublease some of it or use it for storage space and save the cost of a storage unit. This topic is discussed in more detail in Chapter 5.

It is natural to be a bit skeptical about this exercise. If your firm owes hundreds of thousands of dollars, or even millions, it is understandable to wonder how saving a few thousand dollars a month is going to help your firm. The simple answer is that it is the beginning of the process of turning your company around. As illustrated in Table 1-2, cutting several thousand dollars of mission-critical expenditures a month is worth hundreds of thousands of dollars of revenue on an annualized basis. When your staff begins to understand the necessity and value of cost cutting, you might be pleasantly surprised at how many other unnecessary expenditures they recommend cutting. Pretty soon, the team will realize that some expenditures that might have been considered critical to the business were not effective or necessary at all.

Now that you have created your spreadsheet and determined which fixed costs you can eliminate, negotiate with your creditors and landlords. Set up a column in the spreadsheet that includes the proposed start date of getting rid of the location. Also, list the expiration date of the lease.

In addition, determine what your game plan will be if your landlord does allow you to terminate the lease. Before you contact your landlord, figure out how much it will cost your firm to close down the location and how long will it take. If it is clear that there will be significant savings in closing this location, negotiate to get out of the lease as soon as possible. If the landlord doesn't let your firm break the lease, ask for rent forgiveness for as many months as he or she will grant. You don't have much negotiating leverage with your landlord; therefore, any forgiveness should be considered a win.

I have personal experience in trying to get out of a lease that I could no longer afford. When I realized that I was in a bind, I notified my landlord of my situation. I let the landlord know that I was no longer in a position to keep my business running and thus needed to terminate the lease as soon as possible. My landlord was happy for me to terminate the lease, because space in the building was in demand and he could charge the new tenant more for the space I was leasing. Although I got lucky, I helped my situation by being proactive in reaching out to my landlord prior to falling behind in my monthly payments.

If you aren't able to break the your lease or achieve rent forgiveness, examine how you can turn the location around. If you are convinced that there is nothing you can do to turn around the ROI of a specific location, go ahead and shut it down if you will lose less money than keeping it open. Put your energies and the firm's precious resources into winning efforts.

Another area where you may be able to cut costs is with leased equipment. How many company cars, copiers, servers, and so on, are you leasing? Do you really need what you have? If not, try to get out of leasing them. There is nothing wrong with letting vendors know that their company is in jeopardy of losing your firm as a client if they don't work with you. I discuss this topic further in Chapter 5.

Bank Loans

I was once told by a banker friend that, after three missed payments, your loan gets red-flagged for loan committee review. Thereafter, you could be vulnerable to having your collateral seized by the bank, which is the last thing your bank wants to do. It is in your bank's financial interest that your firm be successful so it can make good on its loan obligations. Therefore, it is critical that you be in regular, open communication with your banker. If you have a bank loan that consists of principal and interest payments, ask your bank to give you a reprieve on paying the principal for as many months as possible. Ask for a year and be grateful for what they grant you.

Tip Keep your banker fully apprised of your situation at all times. If you start missing payments without explanation, expect trouble—up to and including the seizure of your collateral. Remember, the bank wants you to succeed and is often willing to help you weather troubled periods.

To get a reprieve on paying the principal on your loan, you have to convince your banker of a few critical points:

- Show your banker an updated set of financials that indicate your firm is either insolvent or close to becoming so.
- Show that you are in the process of developing a plan to turn the company around. Convince your banker that the monies saved by the principal payment reprieve will not be used to pay other past due creditors, but will be used as working capital to restructure the firm's operations. Relate that these actions will help you regain profitability, will give you more cash flow to make bank payments in full and on time, and will ensure that the business stays open to make future bank payments.

Variable Costs

Many firms fall into the trap of believing there is nothing they can do with variable costs because they are necessary to fulfill orders. Although the ingredients or materials may be necessary, there may be ways of purchasing the same item for less. In addition, I have seen poor planning cost companies thousands of dollars simply because a manager did not order a material or ingredient in advance, and ended up paying a 40% to 50% premium on the item because the manager purchased it at a retail store. The defense of such an action is usually along the lines of "We had no choice," "The item was less than a hundred dollars," and so forth.

However, the reality is that these types of purchases add up. They not only cost the company thousands of dollars annually, but they also cost hundreds of wasted person-hours. Sometimes ingredients can be substituted for generic brands without lowering the quality of the final product. Review your ingredient and inventory purchases, then meet with vendor representatives to negotiate a better rate. The vendor may be willing to discount its prices if you provide firm volume commitments as well as aggressive payment terms.

Scorekeeping: Weekly Cash Flow Report

Finding ways to cut costs is an ongoing process, as is tracking the company's cash flow. Someone in your firm, most likely your comptroller or bookkeeper, must be charged with producing a weekly cash flow report, such as the one in Table 1-4.

Table 1-4. Sample Weekly Cash Flow Report

Beginning Cash Balance for Week of 3/03/13			$ 10,000
Collections - 3/03/13 - 3/09/13	Cash Deposits	$ 2,500	
	Check Deposits	$ 12,000	
	Credit Cards	$ 15,000	
Total Collections			$ 29,500
Outflow - 3/03/13 - 3/09/13			
	Payroll	$ 5,000	
	Rent	$ 1,500	
	Electricity	$ 500	
Total Outflows			$ 7,000
Ending Weekly Cash Balance 3/09/13			$ 32,500
Proposed Payments for Week of 3/10/13			
	American Express	$ 6,000	
	Credit Card Balance	$ 20,000	
	Marketing Consultant	$ 5,000	
	Building Maintenance Repairs	$ 10,000	

The report shows the following:

- The beginning cash balance for the week
- A list of all cash inflows (Collections) for the week, whether they be cash payments, checks cleared, or credit card payments received by the bank.

- A list of all outflows for the week, such as what was paid via check or debit card that is going to affect the company's cash balance immediately. By subtracting the cash outflow from the cash inflow, and adding the beginning cash balance, you get your week's ending cash balance.
- A list of invoices for which the comptroller seeks approval to pay the following week.

Most likely, your firm has had enough surprises—self-induced or caused by outside factors. Hence, it is critical that all expenditures not only be approved by management, but also tracked so they are accounted for in your budget. It is also important that your cash inflow be in sync with your account receivables so you are not counting on money that you've already received.

Scorekeeping must be a critical part of your strategy to turn your firm around. A chart that tracks the weekly cash balance illustrates clearly the impact of the recommended changes throughout this book, which can go a long way to regaining some of the confidence inevitably lacking by your management team, not to mention your potential investors and creditors. A weekly cash flow report is not the only report you need to turn your company around, but it is the first and most important one to start with. The rest of the chapters in this book discuss other important reports.

Summary

In this chapter, we reviewed how fundamental it is to get a handle on your company's cash flow to turn your business around. If you don't know where your money is going, then it is hard to determine where you are wasting it. Many entrepreneurs are not good at tracking numbers, much less reading a profit-and-loss statement or balance sheet. Like it or not, if you want to stay in business, you must make scorekeeping your highest priority. It will serve as part of your strategy to buy time so you can determine and solve the systemic problems facing your company.

Working through the exercises recommended in this chapter might be painful, but it is worth it. I'm confident that you will be pleasantly surprised how much money you can save your company by making cash flow management your highest priority. This step is only the first to turn your business around, but it is the biggest and most important.

CHAPTER

2

How to Manage Accounts Payables Better

Coming out of Denial

It is discouraging to look at a long list of vendors to which your firm owes money and not know how and when they are going to get paid. No matter how big the list and the amounts owed, ignoring the issue of past-due payables is only going to make matters worse. This chapter's objective is to help you come up with a game plan to manage more effectively—and eventually reduce and eliminate—your payables in a manner that allows you to increase your cash flow. This strategy buys you the time you need to make other necessary changes in your firm that, over time, help you reduce your payables at a faster rate.

Your Reputation Is at Stake

As long as your business is operating, it is never too late to start focusing on managing your accounts payables better. Reducing your firm's payables decreases your firm's liability. It also improves your firm's credit rating, not to mention your reputation. In addition, it reduces the tremendous amount of stress with which you and your management team are dealing.

Your firm cannot afford to have its critical vendors stop selling you needed materials, services, and/or supplies on credit. You do not want your vendors talking negatively about the firm to other potential vendors, to the firm's customers, or to its competitors, who might try to take advantage of your firm's financial hardship. Furthermore, having a lot of payables can be bad for employee morale, if the employees know that the company's bills are not being paid. Eventually, they'll start to wonder if they won't get paid.

Note When word gets out that you are slow paying your bills, vendors will start avoiding you. Nip this problem in the bud by creating accurate reports to guide you in paying what you can, and talk to your vendors personally. Building relationships now earns you goodwill you can use later when you need it.

Accurate and Current Reporting

The first step in managing payables better requires making sure your accounts payables report is current. Simply stated, this means that the company's department managers need to confirm immediately which goods and services they or members of their department have purchased on credit—approved or not—so these expenditures can be put in to your accounting system.

Wouldn't you already have bills from anyone from whom you purchased goods and services? Not always. Many small service providers, such as IT and marketing consultants, often don't invoice for their work in a timely manner. Hence, it is critical that their services be accounted for. It is extremely frustrating to make difficult budgeting decisions, and even to consider employee layoffs, only to find out weeks or months later that a vendor service was not listed in your budget and now throws your carefully thought-out plans awry.

Tip Find out from your managers and supervisors which services have been performed or goods bought that have not yet been billed. It is essential you know the extent of *all* your liabilities.

Put a Purchasing Approval Process into Place

To avoid any confusion regarding the accuracy of your payables moving forward, management needs to effect immediately an approval process for purchasing goods and services by cash, with credit cards, or by invoice. Simply stated: Determine who has the authority to purchase how much of what goods and/or services before it has to be approved.

The simplest place to start is to limit who has the ability to make purchases on behalf of the company to ensure that prudent purchasing decisions are being made. Start with the company American Express or other corporate cards. Take these steps:

- Cancel immediately all but one credit card. Cut up and shred the rest.
- Determine who is to carry that card and who is to approve any and all requests for purchases.
- Determine who has the authority to make purchases on credit from vendors and the procedure they should follow to inform accounting about an approved purchase.

These recommendations are absolutely critical to the survival of your business and should be implemented as soon as possible.

Create an Accounts Payable Aging Report

After creating the purchase approval process, it is important you create an aging accounts payable report that shows your payables broken down by less than 30 days, 31 to 60 days, 61 to 90 days, and more than 90 days old. See Figure 2-1 for an example of an accounts payable aging summary report.

A/P Aging Summary Example

As of March 1, 2013

	Current*	1 - 30	31 - 60	61 - 90	91 and over	Total
Electric	500	-	-	-	-	500
Phone	-	500	-	-	-	500
Advertising	-	-	5,000	-	-	5,000
Inventory Supplier A	-	-	-	10,000	-	10,000
Inventory Supplier B	-	-	-	-	20,000	20,000
Public Relations Firm	-	-	-	-	3,500	3,500
American Express	-	15,000	-	-	-	15,000
Insurance Renewal	1,000	-	-	-	-	1,000
Accountant	-	1,000	-	-	-	1,000
TOTAL	1,500	16,500	5,000	10,000	23,500	56,500

* Current depends on the terms given by the vendor (e.g net 30 days net 10 etc.)

Figure 2-1. A sample—and simple—accounts payable aging report

It is also critical to categorize your vendors by those from whom you buy regularly and those from whom you make only rare or one-time purchases. The recurring vendors then need to be subdivided into two groups. The first group is classified as those that are critical to keeping the business operating, such as landlords, power providers, telephone providers, and materials suppliers. The second group falls into the nice-to-have category—such as marketing services, subscriptions, and so forth—from which you'll want to purchase after the company is back on track.

Look closely at this latter group. If you don't absolutely have to have the product or service, don't buy it. There will be pushback from various department heads about having their budgets slashed. However, if they cannot make a business case for why the firm should continue to incur the expenditure, strike it from the budget and revisit the desired expenditure after the company is on stable footing.

As mentioned briefly in Chapter 1, I am willing to bet that marketing is an area where you can stop spending money immediately until you have conducted a thorough brand audit. Given your current situation, your marketing is probably not effective. And even if it is, the expected monetary results are not being realized soon enough. Given the fact that you need to preserve cash to stay in business, it isn't wise to add receivables at this early phase of the audit that do not bring in cash, especially if you already have a long list of aging receivables. (I review managing your account receivables in Chapter 3.)

I know some of you may think I am a ruthless finance guy who does not know anything about marketing. On the contrary, my expertise is in strategic marketing. However, I have learned more about finance through the trials and tribulations of being an entrepreneur than from what I learned earning my MBA at The Wharton School. I am writing this book to help you avoid many of my costly mistakes. As mentioned, the bottom line is that selling more of an unprofitable product or service is only going to put you out of business faster.

If you follow the previous recommendations, along with the others made throughout this book, you will start to see that most of your outstanding payables will fall into the 90-days-past-due category. This is because, moving forward, you will be less likely to purchase goods and services for which you cannot pay within the terms stated by the vendor.

Use the Cash Flow Report to Guide Debt Payments

The report shown in Figure 2-2 is an example of a weekly cash flow report. It is critical to use one along with your accounts payable aging report. It will help you determine how much of your outstanding invoices you can pay down or in full. It is also important to know your cash balance at the beginning and the end of each week.

Beginning Cash Balance for Week of 3/03/13			$ 10,000
Collections - 3/03/13 - 3/09/13	Cash Deposits	$ 2,500	
	Check Deposits	$ 12,000	
	Credit Cards	$ 15,000	
Total Collections			$ 29,500
Outflow - 3/03/13 - 3/09/13			
	Payroll	$ 5,000	
	Rent	$ 1,500	
	Electricity	$ 500	
Total Outflows			$ 7,000
Ending Weekly Cash Balance 3/09/13			$ 32,500
Proposed Payments for Week of 3/10/13			
	American Express	$ 6,000	
	Credit Card Balance	$ 20,000	
	Marketing Consultant	$ 5,000	
	Building Maintenance Repairs	$ 10,000	

Figure 2-2. A simple, weekly cash flow report

The report starts with the cash balance at the beginning of the week. Thereafter, there is a listing of the week's cash deposits, checks deposited and cleared, and credit card charges that have cleared. Total these three inflows. Then, list the cash outflows for the week. Include things such as payroll, rent, and any preapproved payments. Now subtract your total outflows from the sum of the beginning cash balance and the cash inflows to determine your ending cash balance for the week.

Your goal: To have the ending cash balance exceed the beginning balance each week. There will be weeks that your cash balance is less because of payroll or rent; however, most weeks your ending cash balance should be higher than the beginning balance.

When you know your cash position for the week, decide which invoices to pay and which to push off to the future. Once again, no invoice should be paid without your approval. Your controller can suggest which bills need to be paid the following week; however, you need to determine what the company can pay based on your current cash and your expected cash inflow from sales collections and accounts receivables. I was in a situation in which I had created a plan to use an expected influx of cash to help generate new, profitable sales, only to find out later that the controller—unbeknown to senior management—used that influx of cash to pay outstanding invoices. That might have felt like the right thing to do at the time, but it was short-sighted because it hindered the company's ability to use that cash to generate even more free cash to pay the remaining debt off even faster.

It is important that your controller run and then send to you by e-mail a cash flow report every week, regardless of whether you have a scheduled meeting with the controller. Your finance people need to develop the discipline of being on top of the company's cash flow. In some instances, you may not be able to review the report for a particular week because of another big problem you are trying to resolve, so it is imperative you make clear that the controller's primary role is to keep score on the company's cash flow. Your job is to develop a strategy and subsequent policies to ensure that the cash is getting its greatest ROI possible, as quickly as possible.

Note Make sure your accountant or controller knows the company's cash position at any moment of the day or week. Your future depends on it.

Reach out to Vendors

Regardless of the category into which you segmented your payables, it is absolutely critical that someone on your team reach out to every vendor that is awaiting payment on an invoice that is more than 30 days past due. Executive management should not hesitate to lead this effort, starting with the most aged accounts. You simply cannot ignore these vendors if you are serious about turning around the firm. If you are nervous about making these calls, create a simple script for you and/or your controller to follow that outlines what you want to say, then stick to the script. Don't make a promise you can't keep.

I believe that honesty is the best policy when speaking to vendors. Ironically, the higher level an executive with whom you speak, the better chance you have of buying more time or working out some type of settlement. Rank-and-file accounts payable personnel are paid to follow the guidelines given to them. Upper management has more flexibility and, in some instances, more appreciation for fellow entrepreneurs who may be going through a difficult time. Let the person you are speaking with know you are committed to doing your best to make progress on paying the outstanding invoice. However, do not overpromise the timing or the amount of your next payment. Your credibility is all the working capital you have left with these vendors.

Different firms, depending on their size and company culture, have different policies regarding how they handle past-due bills. Some firms accept installments of the total balance on a monthly basis if they are confident that your firm can make regular payments. Other firms are willing to negotiate down the total amount due if your firm agrees to pay the agreed-on amount in a more timely fashion. In these instances, the better the relationship you have with your vendors, the more likely they are going to be willing to work with your firm.

I know of one instance when a customer paid down past-due invoices by offering his products and services at a discount. For the most part, however, your vendors want to be assured they are going to get paid, even if it is not as soon as they would like. Larger, more established firms are less patient and are quicker to turn the matter over to a collection agency. In these situations, be prepared for an aggressive person calling your firm monthly, seeking payment and threatening legal action if payment is not made in full by a particular date. Ironically, in this type of situation, your firm may be in an even better situation to negotiate a reduced settlement on a more advanced payment schedule because a collection agency has full authority from the vendor to cut the best deal possible. The agency is motivated to settle, given the fact that it is working off a success fee, usually around 50% to 60% of what is collected.

Tip Consider paying down past-due bills by offering the vendor your goods or services at a discount. Maybe you have something the vendor needs.

Payment Strategy

I know of no science that helps you remit past-due payables when you don't have the cash to pay the balance in full. Coming up with a payment strategy is clearly an art that requires common sense, good judgment, and a little ice in the veins. It is important that you pay all your vendors something every month so they know you are making an effort to pay off your balance (and are not ignoring them)—especially the essential vendors you need to run your business moving forward.

As previously stated, it is critical that no payables be paid without your approval, no matter how much cash is in the bank that particular week. Do not pay sales commissions until payment for those sales is collected. After you have a payment schedule for all your payables, stick to it. As a rule, do not pay more than what you have decided to pay, regardless of how overdue the bills are and how much cash you have. Invariably, you'll get hit with an invoice you had not anticipated and may need the cash for that.

I have found it helpful not only to keep track weekly of what is owed, but also know the weekly count of how many vendors are owed money. The value of keeping track of both of these numbers is to show progress where you can.

Some accounting programs, such as QuickBooks, allow you to compare your budget with actual cash inflows and outflows. Even if you don't have the capability of running such a report, you can still compare your expected cash flow budget to actual profit-and-loss statements for the month. Thereafter, you should make any necessary adjustments to the budget.

Pay off Small Invoices

If and when you have extra cash in the bank, make an occasional exception and pay in full as many of your small vendors as you can as quickly as possible. The amount of time and effort it takes administratively to deal with a $250 or $500 invoice is the same for a $2,500, $5,000 or $25,000 invoice. A phone call from a vendor that is owed $250 is no less time-consuming nor less stressful for the person making the call than it is for a vendor owed ten times as much. The less paperwork and administrative work your accounting department has to deal with, the more time it has to work on tracking down receivables or on tackling other, more pressing projects.

Tip Every so often, pay off a small account in full. You'll save in administrative costs and stress on your accounting staff.

Learn from Past Mistakes

Everyone makes mistakes in business. The key is to learn from your mistakes as quickly as possible, rather than repeat them. Therefore, when you have control of your payables via improved reporting, and when you have put expenditure controls and policies in place, conduct an overall assessment of the progress you have made thus far and take a look back at the decisions that were made that landed you in this mess to begin with.

First, determine which expenditures were worth making and which ones were bad bets from the outset. If management made impulsive expenditures, it needs to think about a more structured way of making better decisions moving forward. I have no doubt your managers will have an opinion of whether the expenditures were prudent. The point of this exercise is not to point blame, but to learn collectively from mistakes to run the business smarter moving forward.

Second, assess your vendors. Some may have delivered what they promised whereas others delivered subpar products or services. In the latter case, don't use those vendors again. In addition, it may be time to cut business ties with so-called loyal vendors who really are not looking out for your company's interest, but solely their own.

Third, look at expenditures that weren't approved and who made them. Determine whether these individuals were aware of your policy on expenditure approval. If they had this knowledge, take disciplinary action if warranted. Reiterate to all employees: *All expenditures must be approved in advanced.* In addition, let your key vendors know in writing the name of the individual at your firm who has the authority to approve purchases, and relay that your company will not be liable for expenditures that are not approved within the new purchasing guidelines.

When employees learn from past mistakes, they tend to work smarter. When managers work smarter, rank-and-file staff members may begin to work smarter as well.

Summary

The beauty of doing the things recommended in this chapter is that you will see immediate results. The payables report, over a period of weeks and months, should look better and better, especially in the 30- to 90-day range. Why? You are purchasing only what you absolutely need, and are spending only what you can pay for. Stay current with your payables moving forward while you improve your margins which will help you reduce your past due payables.

The information provided in this chapter, combined with what you will be learning in subsequent chapters, puts you in a much better position to make good on your payables that are more than 90 days past due. And as the number of your outstanding vendor expenditures shrinks, as well as the total number of overdue payables, your stress will ease as well.

Next up: Managing receivables better.

CHAPTER

3

How to Manage Accounts Receivables Better

Stop Leaving Money on the Table

Similar to having a long list of payables, having a long list of overdue receivables can be discouraging as well. However, receivables need to be viewed as an opportunity to bring in much needed cash as quickly as possible.

This chapter's objective is to help you come up with a game plan to manage and collect your aging receivables more effectively. Considering your situation, collecting overdue receivables must be one of the top priorities of the company. Remember, your firm is not in the business of lending other companies money beyond the agreed-on terms of the initial sale of goods or services. The fact that your firm has a long list of payables should make you even more determined to collect every penny the company is owed so that past-due bills and payroll can be paid in a more timely manner. Let's look at various ways you can do just that.

Accurate and Current Reporting

The first step requires making sure that your accounts receivables report is current. This means that sales reps and customer service department managers need to verify immediately which goods and services were actually sold, delivered, or executed. In other words, confirm all outstanding receivables, then double-check to ensure none are counted twice. Also verify that your firm has sent your clients an invoice for the goods and services they purchased.

Require a Purchase Order from Your Client Before Delivering Goods and Services

As already stated, there are similarities between managing your accounts receivables and managing your accounts payables. To avoid any confusion regarding the accuracy of your receivables moving forward, put into place immediately a requirement for a purchase order from the buyer and/or signature by your clients' senior-level manager when selling goods and services via credit. How much credit and the term length should be determined for each customer—especially for those that have past-due receivables—in part based on their payment history with your company.

Tip To avoid confusion and to leave a solid paper trail, insist that all vendors issue a purchase order for goods bought on credit.

Create an Accounts Receivable Aging Report

While implementing the purchase order system, create an aging report similar to the one depicted in Figure 3-1, which shows receivables broken down by less than 30 days, 31 to 60 days, 61 to 90 days, and more than 90 days old. Generate this report weekly, along with the weekly cash flow report so that they are in sync. Make sure that when payment is received, the respective receivable is removed from the aging receivable report to avoid double booking of revenues and thus false expectations of future cash inflow. The accounts receivable aging report is a similar report to the accounts payables report recommended in Chapter 2, except you are now playing the role of the collector.

A/R Aging Summary

As of March 1, 2013

	Current*	1 - 30	31 - 60	61 - 90	91 and over	Total
Client A		1,000	-	-	-	1,000
Client B	-	-	2,500	-	-	2,500
Client C	-	-	5,000	-	-	5,000
Client D	-	-	-	10,000	-	10,000
Client E	-	-	-	-	15,000	15,000
Client F	-	-	-	-	10,000	10,000
Client G	-	15,000	-	-	-	15,000
Client H	-	-	-	10,000	-	10,000
Client I	1,000	-	-	-	-	1,000
Client J	-	-	-	-	500	500
Client K	-	1,000	-	-	-	1,000
TOTAL	1,000	17,000	7,500	20,000	25,500	71,000

* Current depends on the terms your firm has given to clients (e.g. net 30 days, net 10, etc.)

Figure 3-1. A sample accounts receivable aging report

Reach out to Customers

There will be a lot of reasons why many of your customers are past due on paying their invoices. In some cases, your firm bears indirect responsibility. There is a chance that your firm's point of contact never received an invoice, the accounting department never received the invoice, or the customer misplaced your invoice. In many instances, no one has contacted the company to remind it that an invoice is past due. As in similar situations, the squeaky wheel gets the grease. The firm that owes you money may be having its own financial difficulties. If *you* do not make collecting your much-needed receivables a priority, why would your clients make it a priority to pay you, especially if their business is facing similar challenges to yours?

Tip Sometimes your customer never received an invoice or it was misrouted. A simple phone call can clear up the confusion and get you paid quickly.

In some instances, the accounting department may have received an invoice, but it was not approved by the appropriate people. I saw a case when the person who approved the expenditure was no longer at the company. In this type of situation, accounting has no way to verify that the invoice is valid, because the invoice it did not have a purchase order assigned to it. Regardless of the reason, be more proactive in collecting whatever you can as soon as you can.

Assign Someone to Own the Collection Process

You need to immediately assign someone on your team to be responsible for managing the collection process; otherwise, collections will fall to the wayside—where they probably are right now. I suggest this person be your controller, because he or she is already in charge of managing your cash flow tracking. This does not mean the controller should make all the calls to collect payment of overdue accounts. Rather, your controller should assign who makes which calls, then collect the feedback.

If your firm has a sales team, it should be responsible for the first efforts to recover these outstanding receivables. Sales reps usually have the best relationship with customers. To motivate them to collect past-due bills, make it a policy that sales reps are not paid their commission until the money for the sale has been collected. Not only do sales reps have a greater incentive for making sure the customer pays, but this strategy will make them more diligent in vetting potential new customers.

In some instances, it may be more appropriate for executive management to make direct contact with some customers to collect on aging receivables to impress on the customers how important it is that they address this issue. Regardless of who makes the initial contact, document the feedback given by the customers and forward it to your controller, who should review it and incorporate the information into the weekly status updates.

Tip Get an executive on the phone to collect past-due invoices. It conveys to the other company that getting paid faster is really important to you.

Don't Assume You Will Collect Everything Owed Especially If You Don't Have a Purchase Order

Based on the severity of your company's cash flow situation, when possible, stop providing a line of credit to customers that have receivables 30 days past due. The one exception to this recommendation is for loyal customers that have a pattern of paying their invoices reliably in 45 days, as large corporations often do. Even if there has been an oversight—whether it be a miscommunication or no communication with the customer's accounting department—there is a good chance your firm is not going to get paid in full for the outstanding invoice.

Tip Painful as it may seem, stop providing credit to anyone with an invoice that is 30 days past due. Your sales may drop, but if customers aren't paying, you're not really doing business with them anyway.

Next, I'll say it again to hammer home the idea: Ensure that your reps receive a purchase order—in advance—from their customers for any goods and services delivered. This strategy ensures the order is not only approved, but also that it is in the customer's accounting system. Also, remember that the person who wants your goods and services can be your best advocate in getting overdue invoices paid. If they do not have the ability to help with collections in their company, then tell them they have to pay with a credit card or a company check from this point until the outstanding balances are cleared. This plan will certainly get their attention if they are in real need of additional goods and services that your company provides.

Many of you no doubt feel this approach is too harsh and detrimental to your business. However, your firm cannot afford to operate in any other manner moving forward. Again, selling more unprofitable products—or profitable products on paper that you aren't getting paid for—does not make a whole lot of sense. It is imperative that you hold your ground on the purchase order policy if you are serious about turning around the company. There is a good chance that you may lose some future sales with this approach. However, your number one goal at this juncture is for your business to stay afloat. Furthermore, having a smaller, more profitable business is far more desirable than having a larger, unprofitable business.

Develop a Collection Strategy

Whoever you assign to be in charge of managing the collection process should determine who is going to call every past-due account as soon as possible to determine when each customer is going to send in a payment and/or pay off the entire balance. Whether or to what extent you negotiate with customers about past-due balances depends on how much is owed, how long the balance is past due, your importance to the customer, and your assessment of the likelihood of getting paid in full.

Your controller should get your customers on a payment plan as soon as possible if they cannot pay the past-due balance in full. Regardless of how much is owed and how long it is overdue, ask the customer for a good-faith payment of any amount to be sent in immediately. If your client cannot even send in a fraction of what is owed on the past-due account, you will get a pretty good indication that you're not going to get paid unless you take a more aggressive course of action through a collection agency, or that your client is insolvent and simply does not have the funds to pay you.

Tip Be ready to take payments over the phone with a credit card—even if you don't have a merchant service account. You can always find a friend who has an account who will run the charge on your firm's behalf if you cover the merchant fees for the transaction.

For receivables that are more than 90 days past due, try to collect the money in full. However, if this does not work consider negotiating a settlement amount if the company makes an immediate initial good-faith payment with agreed-on follow-up payment dates. Your firm needs every penny it can collect, but you have to be pragmatic as well. If your customers are also having serious financial difficulties, there is a good chance they don't have the money to pay your invoice in full and are only paying invoices to vendors critical to keeping their company operating. In these situations, consider your receivable a sunk cost and collect whatever you can. If possible, let your customer pay you in goods or services if you can use them. Remember that collection agencies collect up to 50% to 60% of the amount collected in commissions. Therefore, don't hesitate to offer a 25% to 30% discount to help these customers realize they can get this payable off their books if they make a good-faith payment. Just to recap, developing your collection strategy should entail making calls, setting up payment plans and if necessary offering a settlement for accounts over 90 days past due.

Get Your Receivables Factored

Depending on the credit worthiness of your customers, you may be able to have your receivables factored. Factoring firms purchase a company's accounts receivables for a percentage of them. Your banker can probably help recommend a factoring firm. This option can be expensive; most factoring businesses charge something that approximates today's credit card rates. However, this alternative may be worth it if you need the cash *now*. If you cannot get your receivables factored via a factoring firm, ask your investors and board of advisors for recommendations of anyone they know who can provide this service. The rates may vary depending on the amount and/or payment history of your clients with your firm. I personally paid individuals 5% of a $20,000 receivable owed by a *Fortune* 500 company, and it was well worth it at the time. Note that rates are higher for most smaller firms.

Use a Collection Agency

If you have customers that have not responded to your calls and/or e-mail messages despite numerous attempts, turn the account over to a collection agency. If you do not already work with a collection agency, contact one of the same collection agencies that have been calling your firm regarding some of your account payables. Let them know that whatever they collect, less their commission, will go directly toward paying down whatever payables they are trying to get *you* to pay. This strategy can help you in the long run; the collection agency will be more convinced that your firm is serious about resolving its payables and may be more patient with your firm in trying to get the matter taken care of.

Turning some of your receivables over to an agency may seem harsh, but it is a step you must take if customers are ignoring you or not making a good-faith effort to pay down the amount owed to your firm. This step also lessens some of the administrative burden on your employees and ensures a faster payment if, indeed, the client is able to pay the invoice. A collection agency is very diligent about calling customers on a regular basis; it is how they make their money.

Here's how it worked for me once: I had been receiving biweekly calls from a collection agency on behalf of a vendor. I was very direct and transparent with the caller, letting him know the reason that his client had not been paid was because many of my clients had not paid my firm. After getting somewhat annoyed by his twice-weekly calls, I sarcastically stated during one call that I should hire him to collect my receivables. Thereafter, he sent me a simple contract to sign and within weeks he had collected some of my outstanding receivables, which I was able to use to make payments to his client. Although I still owed money to his client, I was able to gain his trust and thereby get him to cease his bulldog tactics, which were only adding stress to an already difficult situation.

Learn from Past Mistakes

As stated in Chapter 2, everyone makes mistakes in business. The key is to learn from your mistakes as quickly as possible rather than repeat them. Therefore, if your firm has a significant amount of past-due receivables, you and your management team must step back and determine what about your company's policies, strategy, and, in some cases, business model must change to rectify this problem moving forward.

I had a client that had a lot of debt and a big list of overdue payables. Ironically, the company also had a long list of overdue receivables. After I learned more about the customers on the receivables list and the reasons they weren't paying on time—and, in some cases, not at all—I realized the situation was more than just a matter of an ineffective policy; the business model was flawed. The client primarily sold its goods via third-party sales agents who sold them to retailers. I recommended that the client get out of the third-party channel and go direct to consumers online who would pay with a credit card, thereby getting rid of a receivables problem. There would be other possible benefits, such as quicker inventory turnover, knowing the actual customer, and receiving invaluable customer feedback directly. At the time, my recommendation seemed like a radical change in the company's business model, and it was met initially with some reluctance. However, over time, executive management realized the value of being a direct retail business rather than a wholesale and/or consignment business.

When evaluating your own business model. Here are a few questions to consider:

- **Are you selling to the right target?** Perhaps your current target channel does not have the ability to pay for your goods or services in a reasonable time period because their own businesses are suffering.
- **Do you have the right payment terms?** Your firm may no longer be in a position to act as a "subprime lender." Hence, tighten your credit terms and the period during which payment is due. In addition,

tighten your policies regarding not selling products and/or services to customers who have accounts that are 30 days past due, until they have cleared their balances. Remember, having a smaller, profitable business is better than having a larger business that is losing money.

- **Do you have an effective collection process?** Do you have regular meetings with your controller, managers, and sales reps to discuss how much their respective customers owe and their game plan to get their customers to pay on time? Who is in charge of follow-up when an invoice becomes past due?
- **Are you selling a product that your customers really want?** "Build it and they will come" is no longer valid in this consumer-driven economy. How do you know there is still a market for your products?

Determining the answers to some of these questions is discussed more in Parts II and III of this book.

Summary

Following many of the recommendations in this chapter will help your cash inflow immediately. The collection of receivables must be a top priority, and thus managed by someone who champions the cause.

Not all of your receivables problems can be blamed on a poor economy. The key is to learn from your mistakes and make the necessary changes to your credit policy, your target clients, and even your entire business model, if necessary. Improving your cash inflow helps you buy time to evaluate these issues and to put your company back on the right track.

Next up: Improving employee productivity.

PART

II

Improving Operations Management

CHAPTER

4

How to Manage Employee Productivity Better

Develop Your Staff to Be Part of the Solution

For many companies, employee payroll is its biggest expense. Unfortunately, it can also be one of the most inefficient. Hence, it is critical that you focus on improving employee productivity as an important component of the strategic plan to turn the company around.

Given all the challenges your company has faced, it is inevitable that employee morale is going to be less than ideal. Management should have a goal of improving morale and productivity, which often go hand-in-hand, by striving for consistency and stability. These two issues are symbiotic and should not be underestimated. When management is not consistent with its strategy and directives, regardless of the reasons, employee productivity is going to drop. When employee productivity drops, so does employee morale. When employee morale is low, productivity tends to decrease. As you can imagine—or as you are probably experiencing—this situation is a negative spiral that needs to be reversed starting at the top.

During a Balance Scorecard workshop I took a few years ago, the instructor, who was a seasoned management consultant, led a discussion that focused on the concept that culture trumps strategy. This concept was not what most executives in the room, including myself, were expecting to hear at a conference focused on strategic planning. However, after a few minutes of everyone reflecting on their professional experiences, there was consensus on the validity of the concept. The sooner you buy in to this concept, the sooner you can start improving employee productivity, because the problems you are facing with your employees are systemic, rather than having to cope with a few disgruntled and/or underperforming employees.

Your employees need to know the truth about your company's predicament. They don't need to know everything, but they do need perspective on how the company got into its current predicament. They also need to know that management is committed to working on a plan to get the firm back on track. Employees must be told what their roles are in being part of the solution.

TURNAROUNDS REQUIRE GREAT PLAYERS AND EXCELLENT COACHES

My friends know me as a basketball junkie, because my 15-year-old son has a dream to play in the NBA. What most of them don't know is that I watch the coaches during practices and games as much as I do the players. I do this because I learn about their management style and the culture they are trying to develop with their team. The great teams don't necessarily have the best players, but they do have the best coaches. These coaches use the best strategies to maximize player strengths and exploit their opponent's weaknesses. They also create teams with great chemistry—in other words, culture—that elevates collective success over individual performance. You don't have to enjoy team sports to understand that this is no less true for managing your workforce.

In addition to defining new or, in most cases, enhanced employee roles, let your staff know what is in it for them if they stick around. Some companies offer their employees stock options, stay-bonuses and opportunities for career advancement, and so on If you think you do not need to do anything for your employees because you think they should be happy just to have a job in a difficult economy, don't be surprised when employee morale and respect for management does not improve regardless of your actions. It is important to underpromise and over-deliver when it comes to setting expectations with your employees. When management makes false promises, it loses credibility in the eyes of its staff and creates a culture of mistrust and cynicism. Hopefully, you and your team are committed to creating a great working environment where your employees take pride in what they do individually and collectively as a company.

Employee Survey

If you have a problem with low morale and productivity, it is critical to garner input from your entire staff regarding how the working environment and morale can improve. This information can be acquired by developing either a written survey or an online survey and by asking your employees to complete it. I recommend an anonymous survey identified by department or division to get as much participation as possible and as much candor as possible. The survey should consist of multiple-choice questions as well as fill-in-the-blank questions. The key is to find out from your employees what they think are the company's key problems—with management, other employees, themselves, and the company's products/services. It is also equally important to find out from the company's employees what they like about the company and what they perceive as the company's strengths.

SAMPLE EMPLOYEE SURVEY

This confidential survey is an important tool to help with the company's planning. It will help determine who we hire, the policies we create, and the training procedures we enact moving forward. It is important that we have a candid assessment from our team regarding how you think management is doing, how you rate your own job performance, how you rate your fellow employees' performance, and how you rate the overall performance of the company. It is critical that you be honest with your assessment.

Personal Assessment

On a scale of 1-10 (10 being "agree completely"), please rate the following:

I like working at the company. ____

I work at the company because I need to earn a paycheck. ____

I work at the company because I would have a hard time finding another job. ____

I clearly understand my role and daily responsibilities. ____

I provide great service to customers and to other colleagues. ____

I work hard and earn my compensation. ____

I work smart and provide value for my compensation. ____

I provide a meaningful contribution to the company's overall performance improvement. ____

I have been supportive of the overall changes executive management is making at the company. ____

I am supportive professionally of my fellow employees regardless of whether I like them. ____

I do a good job of setting a positive example for the company's employees. ____

I am willing to do whatever it takes within reason to improve my performance and to provide better value to the company and its customers. ____

What three things do you do best on behalf of the company?

1. ____________________
2. ____________________
3. ____________________

What are your three biggest areas for improvement in the company?

1. ____________________
2. ____________________
3. ____________________

You may be asking yourself: What's the purpose of this survey and what should I do with the results? The main value of this survey is that, by administering it, you might have already started to change the culture at your firm by letting your employees know you are interested in what they think. In addition, you may get some good insights regarding what they think the underlying problems are in the company.

I recommend using the results of the survey as a benchmark to measure employee morale. You may, however, be in for a reality check of just how frustrated they are working at your firm, and their perceptions regarding their contributions to it. However, if you use only a fraction of the ideas and recommendations made in this book, you will still be pleasantly surprised how your employees answer these questions differently when they are surveyed once or twice a year.

SAMPLE FELLOW EMPLOYEE ASSESSMENT SURVEY

On a scale of 1-10 (10 being "agree completely"), please rate the following:

My fellow employees like working at the company. ____

My fellow employees understand their role and daily responsibilities. ____

My fellow employees work hard and earn their compensation. ____

My fellow employees work smart and provide value for their compensation. ____

My fellow employees make a meaningful contribution to the company's overall performance improvement. ____

My fellow employees are supportive of each other regardless of whether they like each other. ____

My fellow employees are willing to do whatever it takes to improve their performance and provide better value to the company and its customers. ____

What are three things your fellow employees do best on behalf of the company?

1. ____________________
2. ____________________
3. ____________________

What are the three biggest areas of improvement on behalf of the company on which your fellow employees should focus?

1. ____________________
2. ____________________
3. ____________________

Sometimes, employees have an inflated sense of their contribution to your firm. However, they are more grounded when it comes to their fellow employees—hence the value of employees evaluating their colleagues. You get a more candid picture of employee perceptions as well as the areas where self-perception and group perception needs to be bridged.

For example, if all employees thought they were doing a good job but thought their colleagues were not, you could make a fairly accurate assumption that your employees need a lot of training in their responsibilities, as well as a review of the company's policies and procedures to help set appropriate expectations of themselves and their colleagues.

SAMPLE MANAGER ASSESSMENT SURVEY

On a scale of 1-10 (10 being "agree completely"), please rate the following:

My manager likes working at the company. ____

My manager understands his or her role and daily responsibilities. ____

My manager works hard and earns his or her compensation. ____

My manager works smart and provides value for his or her compensation. ____

My manager makes a meaningful contribution to the company's overall performance improvement. ____

My manager is supportive of employees regardless of whether they like each other.

____

My manager is willing to do whatever it takes to improve his or her performance and provide better value to the company and its customers. ____

What are three things your manager does best on behalf of the company?

1. ____________________
2. ____________________
3. ____________________

What are the three biggest areas of improvement on behalf of the company on which your manager should focus?

1. ____________________
2. ____________________
3. ____________________

The value of this survey lies in helping you determine the effectiveness of your managers. If your employees have a low perception of their managers, you have a problem that needs to be rectified immediately. You may have someone in a manager's role who is simply not qualified for that level of responsibility. It may not even be his or her fault; he or she may have been promoted as a result of the predecessor being fired and/or resigning (think of the Peter Principle[1]).

This survey also serves as a red flag for someone you thought was qualified when hired but is clearly not getting the job done in the eyes of your employees. In addition, the survey is a good tool to use to know who is perceived as doing a good job in managing your employees.

EXAMPLE OF EXECUTIVE MANAGEMENT SURVEY

On a scale of 1-10 (10 being "agree completely"), please rate the following:

Executive management has done a good job of explaining the company's direction and strategy. ____

Executive management has done a good job of explaining management's roles and responsibilities. ____

Executive management has done a good job of supporting employees. ____

Executive management has done a good job of holding employees accountable.

____

Executive management has improved the overall morale and direction of the company.

____

Executive management cares about management. ____

Executive management cares about employees. ____

Executive management cares about customers. ____

What three changes would you like to see executive management make?

1. ____________________
2. ____________________
3. ____________________

If executive management doesn't think it bears any responsibility for the company's misfortunes, it should read every one of these types of evaluations. From my experience, a lot of executive managers are clearly out of

[1]Laurence J. Peter believed that, eventually, all managers rise to their level of incompetence.

touch with their managers and the challenges employees face. Executives are so focused on the huge problems the business is facing that they hide in their office, often with the door closed, or stay away from the office and communicate poorly with their staff. Clearly, this can be construed as a sign of burnout, panic, stress, and so forth. It also is a sign that if the founder and/or executive management doesn't change their approach to how they manage their employees, the company is probably not going to make it.

If you don't need your employees, terminate them immediately and quit wasting precious resources. However, the odds are that your employees would not have been hired for a specific role if that role was not needed to help the company achieve its goals and objectives. Therefore, use this survey as a tool to help you determine what changes you need to make to bridge any gaps in communication and expectations you have with your management and staff.

Encourage Innovation and New Ideas

Another way of getting company employees to be part of the solution in turning the company around is to incentivize them to come up with ideas regarding how the company can save money. No CEO or outside consultant can possibly know all the daily actions of every employee in every department. The firm's rank-and-file employees know as well, if not better, than management where the company is wasting money. Hence, it is very effective to create an incentive program for employees to make suggestions on how the company can save money.

Employees who submit suggestions should be thanked by management. Employees whose suggestions are actually implemented should be recognized by management in front of their peers as well as rewarded financially. I often recommend giving $25 to $50 for an idea that saves hundreds of dollars and $100 to $150 for an idea that saves more than $1,000, with no limit to the number of ideas an individual employee can submit. Most of the employees' recommendations will not be genius ideas, nor do they need to be to save or make the company money. In fact, most recommendations that I have seen were no-brainers that should have already been implemented.

However, in most cases, management has been focused on what it perceives as more pressing matters. The reality is that there is no more pressing matter for your business at this phase than managing cash flow. Hence, whether it is a great idea or common sense, thank goodness that someone on your team has taken the time to point out something that can help the firm.

I have seen recommendations regarding saving money on electric bills because the air conditioners in the stores and offices where not being set appropriately after hours and on the weekends during the summer months. I have read recommendations from frustrated managers that have no budget but can't understand why the company is paying for a service it is not even using. I have seen recommendations that point out that a poor-performing store has too many employees whereas a higher performing store does not have enough. One of the best things about this type of program is that it brings out the pride that some of your employees have toward making the business work. It also shows them that good ideas are not only encouraged, but valued.

Tip Do whatever you can to encourage employee suggestions. They know many time and money savers that you just can't see when you're focused on other problems.

Engage Your Employees

If you have two employees who submit the same great idea at the same time, acknowledge and reward both of them. If you have several employees who submit the same idea at the same time, split the reward evenly among them while acknowledging everyone. They key is to get the company's employees engaged as quickly as possible to be able to save as much money as possible and to increase employee morale and productivity.

As a turnaround specialist, I have received pushback from executive management on rewarding employee ideas. Some believe the company cannot afford to pay such rewards. My strong counterargument has always been and will continue to be that the company cannot afford *not* to offer such incentives for employee input. Being pennywise and pound-foolish is not the way to solve your cash flow problems. Such incentive programs are a lot less costly than bringing in consultants to identify money sinks of which your staff has long been aware. A $25 or $150 bonus is a small price to pay for not only usable money-saving ideas, but also for the resulting large boosts in morale. There will be a lot of ideas and recommendations in this book that you won't like. This is one that you should implement immediately regardless of how you feel about it.

SAMPLE GOOD IDEA FORM

In an attempt to improve the overall performance of the business, the company is willing to pay $25 for every good idea that an employee has that will ultimately save the firm money. A great cash-saving idea will earn you $100. There is no limit to the number of ideas you can submit. Please use this form to let management know your idea and its benefit. For example, will your idea help save the company money? Will your idea help the company make more sales? Will your idea help make the company's customers happier? Will your idea improve employee morale? Will your idea improve employee productivity?

Employee Name: ______________________________

Suggestion(s): ______________________________

Setting Expectations and Evaluating Skills

Now that your firm has a clearer understanding of employee perceptions of the company's strengths and weaknesses, as well as their input into where the company can save money, it is important to set and to manage expectations of each employee's core responsibilities. Each employee should have a job description along with short-term objectives. When creating such a job description, it is important to make sure that employees are actually qualified for their respective roles. If they are not qualified, either train them for the role, move them to a more appropriate role, or let them go. If your company is in a sector that has a lot of competitors, there is a good chance that you can find sample job descriptions via the Internet. Don't just use them verbatim, of course; they wouldn't be useful. Use them as guides but adapt them to your unique situation. You can also purchase job descriptions for a nominal fee from a human resource or benefits consulting firm. Thereafter, you can tweak them to meet the unique requirements pertinent to your firm.

Often, the best solution is simply to ask your employees to write down what they do every day. Thereafter, senior management can edit the descriptions with the goal of being as consistent as possible across jobs. Management should also define the criteria by which employee performance will be judged.

It is a fair to ask: Why should employees define their jobs and not management? In a perfect situation, management should have already defined employees' role prior to hiring them; however, in many instances, management is disengaged and does not understand every employee's role. What's more, roles change over time. Hence, the best place to start is to ask employees to document what they do on a daily basis and then determine whether the tasks are appropriate and relevant given the company's current predicament. The job description does not have to be complicated or long; it just needs to capture the daily, weekly, monthly, quarterly, and annual responsibilities for a particular role.

SAMPLE JOB DESCRIPTION FORM

Role/title:

Reports to:

Specific responsibilities:

1. [task 1]
2. [task 2]
3. [task 3]
4. [task 4]
5. [etc.]

Additional responsibilities include but are not limited to

1. Communicating problems to manager/supervisor
2. Creating a weekly status report and/or timesheet
3. Working with other colleagues
4. Following company human resource and safety policies and procedures

The most important aspect of the job description is to set expectations for the employee as well as for management. Job descriptions should be tweaked as the goals and objectives of the company change. As marketplaces evolve and competitors adapt, so should your firm's objectives. Your staff is hired to adapt to these objectives; therefore, their roles and responsibilities may also have to adapt. However, they don't adapt in a vacuum; they need to be discussed and documented. Subsequently, your staff needs to be trained appropriately, and be provided with ongoing feedback.

Weekly Employee Reports

After the job descriptions and objectives are determined, management needs to evaluate employees to ensure each is in the correct position. To ensure better accountability and productivity from each employee, have every employee create a weekly status report. The document can be in the form of e-mail or a handwritten report. Some service companies have employees turn in weekly timesheets to know specifically how their employees spent their time. The value of this is to provide employees with a sense of accountability and to help management gauge whether more staff members are needed. I suggest that this report include, but not be limited to, the following:

1. What did you accomplish during the week?
2. What were the key challenges you faced during the week? Do you have any suggestions for resolving these challenges? If you already solved the problem, how did you do it?
3. What are the key areas of focus for the following week?

It may not be appropriate for every employee turn in a weekly report. Depending on the specific nature of your business, it may be more effective to have your managers touch base with their direct reports to review these issues and then to submit a group report for that particular department.

The report gives managers an idea of what their staff is doing and helps to make sure their efforts are in line with the company's stated objectives. It is also a way for employees to ensure they are documenting their accomplishments and getting feedback from management regarding whether their efforts are on the right track. It is also an opportunity for employees to point out key challenges they are facing that could become bigger problems if ignored.

SAMPLE WEEKLY REPORT

Dear [Manager/Boss—in this case, Apress Publishing]

Please find below a summary of my efforts during the week of 2/4/2013 to 2/8/2013:

My main accomplishment this past week was to complete a first draft of Chapter 4 and to work on Chapter 5.

My main challenge the past week was finding enough time between client meetings to work on Chapter 5.

My goal for the week of 2/11/2013 to 2/15/2013 is to work on making the recommended edits made by the publisher as well as to edit Chapters 1 through 3 before completing a draft of Chapter 5.

Please confirm your receipt of my weekly report and let me know if I am on the right track.

Thanks!

Jonathan

This example gives my publisher an idea of what I worked on that particular week, my challenges that week, and my plans for the following week. It is now the responsibility of my publisher to confirm receipt of my report and to confirm whether I am on the right track according to the goals and objectives of the particular project.

Communication between management and employees can be every company's Achilles' heel. I am amazed how many times I have received weekly reports from staff members who focused their time and efforts on tasks that simply were not a priority and ignored those tasks that should have been a priority. These weekly reports provide an opportunity to bridge communication and to set priorities based on the company's most pressing objectives.

Employee Audit

Employees are not mind readers. The worst feeling for most employees is to be told one thing by their manager one day and then to be told something different the next day. Even worse is when a manager tells an employee one thing related to a particular policy or procedure and then tells another employee something different. For management to provide a more consistent approach to setting and managing policies and procedures, it needs to start by being consistent with the way it manages its staff.

Most founders and CEOs with whom I have worked hate dealing with human resource issues. It is not their specialty, nor is it the reason they wanted to start a business or run a business. In many instances, companies that are facing financial difficulties lay off their human resource director because they think they can get away without having one. Many small businesses have never had a human resource director, and thus the role has fallen on the executive's administrative assistant and, in some cases, the chief financial officer or chief operating officer. It is an area that is ignored until there is problem. This situation is a problem that should be reprioritized as a key action item in turning your business around.

One of the themes throughout this book is to reduce your company's liabilities as quickly as possible to help stabilize the business. Although your employees should be your company's biggest assets, they can also be its biggest liability as a result of failure in matters related to safety, customer relations, employee relations, employee morale, and so forth. Therefore, for you to leverage your staff more effectively, you need to make human resources a higher priority.

Whatever problems you face at work and at home, you can be sure many of your employees face the same ones, if not more, with a lot fewer financial resources at their disposal to help work through them. Regardless of the size and number of problems your firm is facing with customers, lenders, vendors, and investors, you are never relieved of following employment laws or treating your staff with professional respect and fairness. It is critical to view your employees as allies and not as enemies. Therefore, the first step in creating a safe and fair work environment is to do an audit of your employees the way a human resource professional might.

Safety

The first priority related to employees should be in the area of safety. Say you're reading this book at your office and an employee down the hall or in the warehouse is having a heart attack and needs to go to the hospital. Do you know who to contact in his family? Who his doctor is? His preferred hospital? When you are told the employee's name, do you know what he looks like? If your employee is a recent immigrant who does not speak English well, can you understand what he is telling you? If you answered no to any of these questions, your first step in reducing your employee liability issues is to develop a master emergency contact list for every person working in your business—full-time, part-time, hourly, salaried, and executive employees. The obvious place to start your list is to consult your payroll report.

This list is a confidential company document for senior management only. A sample is presented in Figure 4-1. The list should include the following:

1. Legal first and last names
2. Nickname
3. Home and cell phone numbers
4. Personal e-mail address
5. Emergency contact and relationship to the employee
6. Emergency contact's number
7. Preferred hospital in the event of an emergency
8. Employee picture

Last Name	First Name	Position	Cell Phone	Home Phone	Personal Email	Emergency Contact	Relationship	Emergency Contact's Number	Picture
Lack	Jonathan	Consultant	(713) 123-7777	NA	jlack@abc.com	Jon Doe	Brother	(713) 123-4567	

Figure 4-1. Sample emergency contact list

Create this list in Excel and either send it by e-mail to all of your employees or print it out and circulate it. Employees can take pictures of each other with a camera phone, or someone can use a digital camera to take each other's picture. When you have every employee's contact information, date the document and give copies to key managers. You will be glad you did; you never know when an employee is going to have an emergency.

A few weeks after I had a client company do this, a worker in commissary cut her finger. She did not speak English very well; however, because she had filled out her emergency contact information, the company was able to call her emergency contact—who spoke English fluently—and who quickly came to the office to take the employee to her doctor.

Employee History

The next step in conducting an audit of your employees is to know their employment history at the firm and elsewhere. This would include meeting notes and key emails regarding positive or negative performance issues. This type of documentation protects both the company and the employee, because records of what was said when can be important in clarifying expectations and/or resolving disputes. Therefore, an employment file should be created and updated periodically for every employee.

Hard as it is to believe, many companies do not keep such employee files. I have consulted for firms that did not have files on their employees, which contributed to low employee morale because employees claimed they were made promises by management that could not be confirmed. In addition, management claimed it had given warnings to certain employees, which also could not be confirmed. Not having records of employee work status (in other words, full time, part time, hourly, or salaried) and pay increases can also create havoc when trying to determine the appropriate merit raise for a particular employee.

Employee files do not have to be elaborate. They should contain, but are not limited to, the following:

1. Original employment application
2. Any and all background reports run on the applicant (such as criminal, credit, employment verification, and so forth)
3. Weekly reports
4. Write-ups for misbehavior and/or accolades
5. Performance reviews

Review Employees Annually

Given the problems your firm is facing, it probably has not conducted performance reviews for quite a while. When the firm is in a position to do so, it should conduct these reviews; however, the process of reviewing employees needs to be well thought out in advance.

Employees need feedback regardless of whether there is money in the budget for raises and/or bonuses. Pick a date or milestone to achieve, after which the company will get back on track having regularly scheduled performance reviews. This action puts every employee back on the same schedule for overall planning purposes.

Note It is not within the scope of this book to offer advice on reviews. Just understand that they are important from a legal point of view and—conducted correctly—are a good way to improve employee performance over time.

Employee Manual

It is important that management review the employee manual to determine whether policies and procedures are still relevant. If a manual does not exist, one needs to be created. There are many consultants and software programs that can help you do this.

One of the tools management can use to create a culture of consistency and stability is an employee manual that states the company's policies and procedures. Your firm does not need to have a human resource director to create a manual if you don't already have one. Many payroll services offer boilerplate manuals that allow you to fill in the blanks of the specific details of standard policies and procedures covered in employee manuals.

Here is a bare-bones outline for a policy manual. Most cover many more topics.

1. Safety policy and procedures
2. Work hours and overtime policies
3. Vacation, holiday, and time-off policies
4. Benefits and health insurance policies
5. Compensation policies
6. Training policies
7. Antidiscrimination and sexual harassment policies
8. Drug, smoking, and alcohol policies
9. Performance review and discipline policies
10. Grievance/open-door policies
11. Termination and separation policies

After completing and/or updating the manual, management should review it with all employees and have each one sign a one-page acknowledgment that they received a copy of the manual, read it, and are committed to abiding by the stated policies and procedures. The signed copy goes into the employee's file. Every new employee, moving forward, should receive a copy of the manual and sign the acknowledgment form.

Note The employee handbook or policy manual should be reviewed by management during its annual planning period, and should be reviewed with employees on an annual basis.

It may be a pain or appear to be a waste of time to develop or update such a manual. However, by reviewing the new and/or revised manual with your staff, you are sending a message that you don't want to manage by double standards and that you are documenting what every employee is entitled to regarding benefits. Your firm does not have to have a human resource director to do these basic but critical tasks. An employee manual can go a long way toward helping to manage expectations.

Last word: When you have a manual, reiterate that that all employees including management follow its policies. Employees launch lawsuits based on deviations from stated policies or by inconsistent application of them.

Ongoing Communication

Do not assume that your employees understand your business model and the contributions of various departments and divisions in your business. Also, do not assume that your employees have an understanding of what information is confidential and is not to be discussed outside the work environment. Therefore, it is critical to establish ongoing, face-to-face communication with your employees to ensure that they understand the policies stated in the manual. One way of managing expectations placed on your employees is to have weekly or biweekly departmental staff meetings. These meetings should be used as a vehicle to determine the issues your staff is facing as well as an opportunity to reinforce company objectives and to elaborate on current initiatives.

These meetings can be as short as 30 minutes, but no longer than 90 minutes, to maximize their effectiveness. Conduct joint department meetings, quarterly divisional meetings, and, depending on the size of your firm, a semiannual all-employee fun event. These types of gatherings can be both informative and fun. The aim is to give your entire staff a better understanding of and appreciation for the intricacies of the business as well as the importance of their individual role as well as their department's role in the overall success of the company's mission and vision.

Whoever is in charge of these meetings should give some thought in advance regarding the meeting agenda and whether employees need to do anything to prepare for the meeting. Have someone take notes at the meeting. Identify who is responsible for what follow-up actions and the target date for completion. Then, distribute the minutes or action list after the meeting.

Group Outings Help Bond the Employee Family

Host a fun outing with all your employees as soon as possible. It is important that they know that management is doing everything possible to turn the company around and that they are appreciated individually and collectively. Do not underestimate the goodwill you can create by sharing a meal with your employees and their families, as well as by having fun together. Options include putt-putt golf, penny arcade, bowling, a picnic, and so on. I have helped organize these types of outings and often notice a bump in employee morale the following week. These events don't have to be expensive or fancy—just fun. In addition, you will learn a lot about your staff—in part by who shows up and who does not.

Summary

Never underestimate the importance of internal communications with your team. The old adage of tell them what you are going to tell them, tell them, and then tell them what you told them is valuable to a firm that is experiencing difficulties. Remember, culture trumps strategy. Although culture starts with leadership it is impacted by everyone that works at your company. Thus, *every* employee should be viewed as—and challenged to be—an important part of the solution to turning the company around. Conducting an employee survey is a great way to get valuable feedback on an employee's perception of their performance and morale, those of their colleagues and of their manager. Getting your employees more engaged in the turn around process is critical. This can be achieved in part by encouraging innovation and new ideas, by setting expectations and evaluating skills, and by keeping your employees accountable in part by requiring weekly updates on their progress. Throughout this entire process you want to be as consistent as possible with policies and rules. Hence, it is important to develop and/or update an employee manual with the company's policies, rules, and benefits. Finally, ongoing communication and reinforcement of the company's key goals and objectives is as important as keeping employee morale high.

In Chapter 5 we will focus on how to manage technology, facilities, and manufacturing better.

CHAPTER

5

How to Manage Technology, Facilities, and Manufacturing Better

Improving Utilization Is Critical

Just as the goal of Chapter 4 was to improve the overall productivity of employees, the goal of this chapter is to improve the overall productivity of your technology, facilities, and manufacturing, which not only contributes to your operating margins, but also to employee productivity. These three areas of your business are tools that help it achieve optimum success. If the tools are not needed, get rid of them. If they are needed but are not being used effectively, change your approach to leverage them more fully. Most important, stop ignoring them and assuming they are costs you just have to deal with. You need to treat your technology, facilities, and manufacturing areas as investments that get a positive return.

Auditing Your Technology

Your business, like all businesses, is becoming ever dependent on technology. When the technology at your company is working, you and your employees are probably not even thinking about it. This latter point is probably especially true given the other challenges your business is facing. However, when technology is not working, regardless of the reason, it can cripple the productivity of your entire staff and impact your sales significantly, which you cannot afford to lose. One of the goals of this chapter is to help you come up with a pragmatic and cost-effective approach to reducing your current technological vulnerabilities and, subsequently, leverage technology better to help your business run more efficiently.

If your firm does not have a full-time or an outsourced third-party IT staff member, you need to designate someone on your staff to conduct an audit of all your IT equipment as soon as possible. If you do not have someone qualified on staff, hire an outside consultant. Whoever conducts the audit should follow a process similar to what is illustrated next. A third-party experienced consultant may have a different audit template, which is fine, as long as it covers the same ground.

The first step in taking a technology audit is to identify

1. The various types of technology you have
2. The condition and status of each piece
3. What could go wrong with each piece of equipment
4. A plan of action when something does go wrong
5. A maintenance schedule to help prevent something from breaking down
6. New equipment needs

The next step is to document policies and procedures as they relate to technology use, including what should be done and who should be notified when something is not working correctly. This effort, like the others reviewed in this book, should be communicated appropriately to management and staff. In addition, the maintenance schedule and wish list of new equipment should be incorporated into the company's planning budget. The whole process is outlined in Figure 5-1.

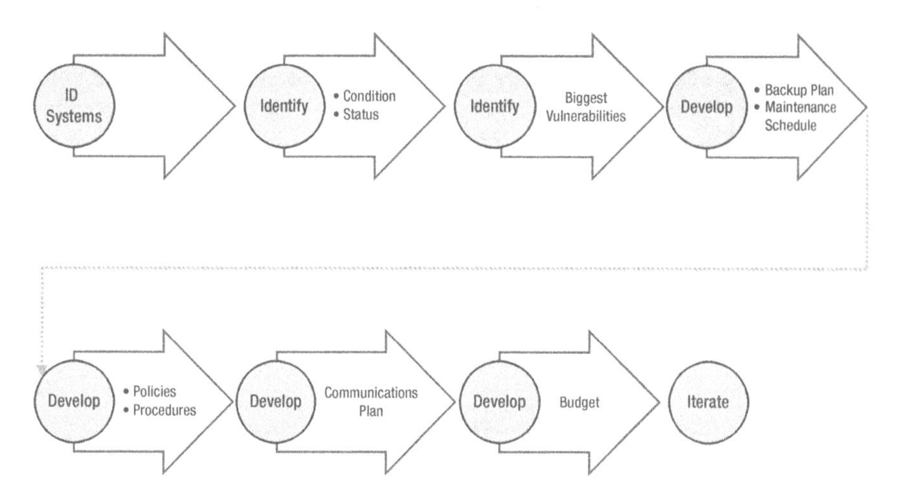

Figure 5-1. Equipment evaluation process flow

It may be a natural reaction as well as a valid point to say that your technology is the least of your company's challenges. However, a fix-it-when-it-breaks approach will most likely cost the company more time and money in the long run. Identify potential problems before they occur.

Tip Plan to conduct preventive maintenance. Waiting for something to break down before you fix it is a sure money loser. Besides losing sales, your repairs will cost more, too.

The goal of an audit is to

1. Help find ways to save time and money immediately
2. Develop a list of affordable actions to be taken that can improve efficiency and reduce downtime
3. Develop a phased approach to better technology solutions that are tied into other operational and financial milestones as part of the overall strategic planning process

It should not take you very long to do an audit as long as you have someone dedicated to the task and focused on making it a top priority.

Table 5-1 is an example of how you might track your audit. Start with listing the specific pieces of technology equipment in the first column and who, if anyone, is using it. For example, count the number of cell phones for which the company is paying and list everyone who is using one. Sit down with your accounts payable person/controller to confirm just exactly what is being paid for every month. You may be surprised to learn that the company is paying for phones that were used by employees who have not worked at the firm for months.

Table 5-1. Technology Inventory Form

Equipment Type	Total Number/ No. of Total	Version/ Serial/ Licence Number	Status (Excellent, Adequate, Needs Replacing)	Required Maintenance Schedule	Recurring Costs/ Replacement Fee	In-house/ Outsourced	Replacement Cost	Necessity/ Luxury
Cell Phone	4							
President's	1 of 4							
CFO's	2 of 4							
COO's	3 of 4							
VP Sales'	4 of 4							
PCs	10							
President's	1 of 10							
CFO's	2 of 10							
COO's	3 of 10							
VP Sales'	4 of 10							
Admin	5 of 10							
Support - 1	6 of 10							
Support - 2	7 of 10							
Staff - 1	8 of 10							
Staff - 2	9 of 10							
Staff - 3	10 of 10							
Phone System	1							
Servers	1							
T-1 Line	1							
MS Office - enterprise	1							
Security Software - enterprise	1							

The second column should have the total number in each category. The third column should have some type of serial number and/or the license number of each piece of equipment or software package tied back specifically to each unit/user. The fourth column should have the status of a piece of equipment. Keep the status rating simple by using variables such as *excellent*, *adequate*, or *needs replacing*. For the audit to be objective, the person conducting the audit does not worry about replacement costs; they are what they are. It is management's role to decide whether the company is in a position to act on the auditor's recommendations.

The fifth column should list the monthly recurring costs for a piece of equipment and/or its replacement cost. This information is important in determining whether it makes more sense to outsource the management of a piece of equipment to a firm that is able to purchase it cheaper than your firm and that is more skilled in maintaining it. The sixth column should list an appropriate maintenance schedule, if required, for each piece of equipment. The seventh and last column should list whether the service is in-house or outsourced. For example, your firm may have a server room or you may be using a third-party's server.

For the equipment and/or services that are outsourced, the company should consider whether it makes sense to get a bid from another service provider to determine whether you can either lower costs and/or improve performance. Your audit may indicate that you have equipment that is not necessary to your company's productivity. If so, get rid of it. For example, you may have too many leased copiers, unnecessary maintenance agreements, too many cell phones, and so on. It is important to note that no amount of savings is too little. It all adds up. As mentioned in Chapter 1, a few hundred dollars saved monthly is equivalent to thousands of dollars of new, recurring revenues.

You may also find out that, for a nominal cost, you can invest in a new piece of equipment—such as a laptop or iPad—that improves productivity immediately. It may pay for itself in a matter of weeks. I vividly recall that, during the process of conducting a strategic plan for a client, I met a warehouse manager who worked in a separate location from the corporate headquarters. This gentleman was responsible for tracking hundreds of thousands of dollars of inventory on his laptop. He was extremely appreciative of his job. He was also very loyal to the company and concerned about the company's cash flow situation. He was so concerned that he did not want to ask for a new laptop even though his screen was broken off its hinges and would flicker on and off. The financial consequences of reading inventory incorrectly because of a defective screen far outweighed the few hundred dollars it cost to purchase a new laptop. I spoke with the CEO about this matter and the man had a new laptop within a week.

Tip Spend money when you need to. Skimping on essential technology costs you more in the long run than buying a new, needed product in the first place.

Leverage Your Technology

Now that you have conducted an audit of what you need and do not need, it is important to make sure you are maximizing the use of your technology. The person in charge of your audit should also be in charge of ensuring you are maximizing the productivity of each piece of technology.

This task requires a time investment to interview members of your staff who are using each piece of equipment the most to get a better understanding of what they are trying to accomplish by using it. When the auditor knows the staff's objectives, he or she can assess more effectively if the equipment is being underused. If the equipment *is* being underused, your auditor should develop a simple plan of action to rectify the situation, such as talking to the representative of the company that sold and/or leased the equipment to you to determine how to make the most of it. You can also go to the respective company websites of the various equipment manufacturers and search for a training video for the equipment to leverage its technology. If a manufacturer video is not available, search YouTube for a video that a competitor may have produced that may be similar enough to be of value.

Auditing Your Facilities

Conducting an audit of your facilities is a parallel process to conducting an audit of your technology. Your goal is to understand what you have, where you are vulnerable to risks, and how you can reduce waste and improve efficiency. Doing so contributes to the overall performance improvement of the company.

Have the chief operating officer conduct the facilities audit. If you don't have one, assign someone to conduct this audit who understands the production flows in the company. If you have an internal person conducting your technology audit, that person may also be a good choice to conduct your facilities audit as well. The audit processes are similar, and the auditor can draw on his or her technology audit experience to help develop an effective facilities audit.

The first step in taking a facilities audit is to identify

1. Each specific facility
2. Whether you lease it or own it
3. Terms of the lease or terms of finance
4. A plan of action if the facility becomes unusable
5. A maintenance schedule
6. A utilization rating

Given that you are probably leasing your various facilities, it is important that you determine whether you really need each one. If you are leasing retail space, it is important to know whether you are making money at each store. If you are losing money at a location, and you do not think you can turn your store around with better operating procedures and/or a more effective marketing campaign, shut down the store as soon as possible and get out of your lease.

If you are renting warehouse or storage facilities, determine the percentage of the space that is being used. If you are paying for space you are not using and do not foresee making full use of it in the next 6 to 12 months, reduce the underused space by consolidating the spaces you are leasing. If you have a large corporate office that is underused, sublease some of your office to sole proprietors on a monthly basis.

Tip Take a hard look at each facility you own or lease. Most likely, there is excess space you can put to better use or can sublet to someone who can.

Charting Facilities Use

As illustrated in Table 5-2, start by creating an inventory of your facilities with some basic, but important, information. The first column should list the name of each facility your firm leases and/or owns, including corporate office space and each store, warehouse, storage unit, and manufacturing facility. In the second column, list the monthly payments for each facility. In the third column and fourth columns list the square footage of each facility and how much of it is being used. In the fifth column, list a disaster contingency plan if that facility is no longer usable as a result of a storm, pipe leak, earthquake, and so on. In column 6, determine whether the facility is really needed or whether it is an unnecessary luxury given your current cash constraints. In column 7, determine the maintenance schedule the facility needs, such as air-conditioning and heating servicing, window washing, office cleaning, floor waxing, painting, and so forth. Also, list who within your organization is responsible for making sure the maintenance schedule is followed.

Table 5-2. Sample Facilities Use Chart

Location	Monthly Payments	Lease Terms	Square Footage	Current Utilization	Disaster Contingency Plan	Needed/ Luxury	Maintenance Schedule
Corporate Office							
Store 1							
Store 2							
Store 3							
Warehouse 1							
Warehouse 2							
Storage Unit 1							
Manufacturing Facility							
Manufacturing Facility							

Reducing the overhead of underused facilities may be a difficult decision for you to make psychologically because it appears that you are contracting your business rather than expanding it. However, the fact is that if you can get rid of wasteful, recurring monthly expenses, your margins are going to increase, which gives you a greater cash flow to use to improve the other aspects of your business. You can always rent more space when your firm is back to where you want it to be. The key now is to ensure you stay in business.

Improve Your Manufacturing Process

Improving the production of your products, whether outsourced or manufactured internally, is critical to your firm's success, and it should be an ongoing process. When I searched Amazon for books on how to manufacture products, I got more than 64,000 results. There is so much information on how to improve the process of manufacturing products that it can be hard to know where to begin. The key is to approach the issue in a pragmatic manner. Rank your approach to improving your manufacturing process by setting some goals and objectives that can be achieved quickly. The following sections will help you start the process.

Goal 1: Develop a Plan to Sell Your Old Inventory

Your company desperately needs cash to stay in business. Your firm also probably owes your manufacturers and/or suppliers money. Therefore, to help achieve goal 2 (next section), you need to develop a game plan to sell old inventory that, for whatever reason, is not selling. What you paid for this inventory is irrelevant. Someone will purchase it for the right price. Be prepared to negotiate with an interested buyer.

In addition to developing a game plan to sell this inventory, do a quick assessment of why the inventory has not sold. Is the product out of style, priced too high, defective, the wrong color? Learn from this experience so your product planning improves and becomes more effective during your next product development cycle.

Note No matter how obsolete you think your inventory is, someone will take it off your hands for a certain price. Even if you sell it for a pittance, you won't need to store, insure, or think about it anymore.

Goal 2: Keep Your Manufacturers and/or Suppliers Happy

Although you may owe money to your manufacturers and/or suppliers, you have very little chance of ever paying them back and/or staying in business if they do not provide you with new inventory and/or supplies on some type of extended line of credit. Given this reality, it is critical that you be transparent with your manufacturers and suppliers. In addition, maintain regular communication. Regardless of where your manufacturers are located, visit them as soon as possible to request, face-to-face, a new line of credit. If they decide not to extend you more credit until your outstanding payables are resolved, do some legwork and visit a local backup manufacturer who may be willing to extend you a line of credit to get your company's business. It is very common for similar types of manufacturers to be located in the same city and/or region.

If your company is a large one and you decide to send someone to meet with your manufacturers in your stead, consider sending the manager/point person who interacts regularly with your manufacturers and suppliers. Be aware that you risk the possibility of your manager leaving the firm with no else at the firm having a relationship with your manufacturer. Not having your own relationship with your manufacturers makes your company more vulnerable to event risk. Your visit sends a signal that you are serious about improving your working relationship.

Do some basic due diligence on your manufacturers and their country before your trip so you are prepared to accommodate their cultural business norms. If you have an international broker that found you the manufacturer, ask that person for insight on the people you will be meeting to help you prepare more effectively for your meetings.

Goal 3: Explore Ways to Reduce Production Costs Immediately

When meeting with your manufacturers or suppliers, it is imperative that you brainstorm together regarding how your firm can reduce its production costs beyond your own labor management. There may be elements in your products that are not necessary to meet your customers' expectations. You may be paying for an overkill product with features that are simply not appreciated by your customers. Don't be afraid to explore these options with your manufacturers. The worst thing that can happen is that your premise may not be correct and you have to reinstall the elements you eliminated.

You may be able to substitute elements or ingredients in your products with generic versions. This is especially relevant in the food business.

Although you are strapped for cash, you may pay be able to get better pricing with more aggressive payment terms. If this is a significant amount of money, you may have to have to be a bit stingier with your other payables and more aggressive with your receivables collection so that you can increase your margins, which are going to provide you with more cash to stay in business. Also, you may be able to get better terms by modifying production or delivery schedules.

Goal 4: Reduce Your Product Selection

I am amazed by how many clients with whom I have worked that have no clue what their margins are for their respective products. They know the aggregate margins, but this knowledge does not provide any insights regarding which products are profitable and which ones are losing money. It is important not to be fooled by revenues alone. You can have a product with lots of sales and be losing money on it. In addition, you can have a product with modest revenues but high margins.

You are not in business to lose money. As soon as you determine the margins for each of your products, stop producing the ones that are losing money. No exceptions! You are going to have customers who will be upset; however, you need to figure out how to make these products profitable before you put them back in circulation. Also, figure out how to make the products that are barely profitable more profitable. Exploiting your high-margin products is not a production issue but a sales and marketing issue, and I cover this topic in Chapters 8 and 9.

HOW TO FIGURE PRODUCT MARGINS

Knowing your margins on each of your products and services is critical to managing your operations better. As Table 5-3 illustrates, looking at your financials based on averages does not give you enough information to manage your business more effectively. The second column to the left shows that this company is making a 3% net profit. However, when each product's costs are broken down individually, you can see that only one of the four products is actually profitable. Products 1 and 3 are losing money. Product 2 is breaking even. With this type of information, the company can now focus on fixing the problems with its products. If the company discontinues the unprofitable product immediately, the other products will have to absorb the indirect costs, which make all but the fourth product unprofitable.

Table 5-3. Sample of Margin Breakdown by Individual Product

	Total	%	Product 1	%	Product 2	%	Product 3	%	Product 4	%
Revenue	$10.00	100%	$1.00	100%	$2.00	100%	$3.00	100%	$4.00	100%
Direct Expense										
Labor	$3.20	32%	0.40	40%	0.70	35%	0.90	30%	1.20	30%
Supplies	$4.00	40%	0.50	50%	0.80	40%	1.50	50%	1.20	30%
Total Direct Expense	$7.20	72%	0.90	90%	1.50	75%	2.40	80%	2.40	60%
Indirect Expenses (Marketing, Rent, Insurance, etc.)*	$ 2.50	25%	$ 0.25	25%	$ 0.50	25%	$ 0.75	25%	$ 1.00	25%
Earnings Before Interest & Taxes (EBIT)	$ 0.30	3%	$ (0.15)	-15%	$ 0.00	0%	$ (0.15)	-5%	$ 0.60	15%

* Indirect expenses are prorated across product lines based on a percentage of revenues

It is critical that you know and understand your numbers. In this example, the company is better off trying to lower its direct cost or raising its pricing—something that might be easier than trying to decrease its indirect costs further.

The first step in determining the margins on your products is to have an accurate record of their individual sales. Thereafter, it is important to determine the labor cost to develop each product as well as the supplies/materials costs for each product. The revenues, less your labor and supplies/materials costs, is your gross margin. Your net margins, or EBIT (earnings before interest and taxes), is calculated by adding your indirect expenses (insurance, marketing, rent, and so forth) to your direct expenses and then subtracting that number from your revenue total. In Table 5-3, I prorated the indirect expenses based on each product's revenue as a percentage of the total revenue.

Goal 5: Consider Joining a Buying Co-op

Many small companies simply do not have the buying power to get favorable pricing from suppliers. Seek out an industry buying co-op that you may be able to join, which may be as simple as searching for one with Google. If this doesn't work, contact your industry trade association for assistance. Network at industry trade shows to find out if there is an appropriate co-op for your business. This strategy allows you to get more competitive pricing because you will be part of a larger buying group.

Goal 6: Evaluate the Efficiency of Your Equipment

Are you using equipment to produce your products that is old and out of date, thereby slowing your product process and increasing your labor costs? Is it possible to buy newer components, even if used, that will allow you to produce more products and reduce labor costs? If you are able to quantify your savings potential, it may be more cost-effective to buy or lease a newer but used piece of equipment that will more than pay for itself, which helps you to increase your margins. You may want to engage an equipment broker to help you figure out your best options.

Goal 7: Leverage and, Subsequently, Reduce Your Scraps

Inevitably, there is supply waste in the production process of any product. What, if anything, can you do to leverage the scraps? Can you reissue them for the same product? Can you make another product out of the scraps with nominal additional labor costs?

Explore how you can improve the production process to reduce your scraps. Can better planning improve your supply waste? Can better staff training improve the production process? I saw, firsthand, a CEO state emphatically that his employees were making products in the most efficient manner possible. After some study, it was clear that he had no clue that the entire production process was riddled with inefficiencies. Why? He was out of touch with what was happening in his company.

Goal 8: Never Stop Trying to Improve the Production Process

Although there is no guarantee of success, I find it hard to believe that your firm could not make significant progress by implementing the recommendations in this chapter that are relevant to your company's situation.

Similar to the other suggestions made throughout this book, after you and your team start thinking out of the box, you will be start changing your company culture to being more aggressive and creative at problem solving. Improving your manufacturing process must be an ongoing process for your firm to compete in the digital global economy, regardless of your company's sector. The key is to keep pushing on improving your production process in the context of the other major challenges you are dealing with so that you are getting the biggest bang for your buck, time, and energy. In Chapter 6, I show you how to put your manufacturing challenges in context with the other challenges the company is facing to help you prioritize which battles to fight.

Summary

Improving the use your technologies, facilities, and manufacturing needs to be a critical component of your strategic planning effort to turn your business around. Conducting audits of your technologies and facilities to determine what you need and what you don't need is imperative. Do not underestimate the importance of the savings you can find during these audits. Understanding replacement costs and maintenance scheduling is critical as well.

It is also important to improve your manufacturing process. Although improving production is an ongoing process, setting short-term objectives to save money by trying to increase margins is absolutely a top tier priority. Develop a plan to sell your old inventory. Focus on keeping your manufacturers and/or suppliers happy. Explore ways to reduce production costs immediately. Reduce your product selection. Explore joining a buying co-op. Evaluate the efficiency of your equipment. Leverage and eventually reduce your production waste. Last, never stop improving your production process.

CHAPTER

6

How to Manage Process Flows Better

Cross-Departmental Collaboration Is Critical for Improved Operational Efficiency

This chapter's objective is to help you manage your overall operational process flows—such as sales, marketing, and product development—better. This may be an entirely new concept for you; however, it should be a central focus of your efforts to turn your company around. We have discussed how important it is that you and your team focus on working smarter. One way of working smarter as a company on a daily basis is through a commitment of identifying your key process flows, defining them, and then constantly trying to refine them.

As important as it is to develop a strategic plan, it is equally important that you develop a process flow strategy, which ultimately will enable you to implement your strategic plan more effectively. In a company culture that is heavily personality-centric, developing a process flow is not going to be easy—in part, because it is not necessarily intuitive.

A personality-centric company culture revolves around the idiosyncratic behavior of the CEO. As a CEO or owner of your own business, you may be asking: What is wrong with running the business the way I want to? It's a fair question that merits a thoughtful response. If your management style is based on gut intuition or how you feel at a given moment, you run the risk of sending contradictory directives to your staff. In addition, you also run the risk of your staff becoming passive out of fear that whatever initiative they would like to take may be undone by you.

A process-oriented culture, on the other hand, revolves around decisions being made based on best practices, consistency, and empowerment of your staff to take initiatives within their respective roles and responsibilities, assuming they can tie them back to set goals and objectives.

When you start to understand the logic behind this strategic tool, you will catch on very quickly. If you can lead your management and staff into buying into the logic behind it, you will have made tremendous strides in changing your company culture to one that is more process- and metric-driven. You will also see many of the metrics moving in a positive direction, especially the reduction in your labor and marketing costs.

It is important to note that you start the practice of managing your overall process flows as part of your strategic planning. However, you should have a realistic expectation that, given all the other major challenges with which your company is dealing, this task may take several months to initiate at best, and most likely a full calendar year to instill, along with an annual review. The key objective of this exercise in process flow is to give you a framework from which you can manage your business more effectively and more efficiently. As a result, you will improve your margins, your cash flow, and, ultimately, your profitability.

Developing Process Flows

You may recall that, back in Chapter 4, I discussed the importance of every one of your employees having a clear understanding of his or her role and responsibilities. Developing a process flow will help them determine not only how they should be implementing their responsibilities but also how they should be working with their colleagues. Having the flow recorded is especially important in case a key employee leaves your firm. If documented properly, an employee who resigns won't be leaving with as much institutional memory. The replacement, whether it be a new hire or someone from within the company, will not only have a job description with roles and responsibilities already defined, but will also have a process flow developed that explains how and when to interact with colleagues. Conducting this exercise also helps you determine whether you have staff in some areas where they are not really needed. In addition, you might find areas in which another employee is needed to bridge a workflow gap.

Tip Document your processes, in part, to mitigate the effect of important people leaving the company and taking institutional memory with them.

At first glimpse, Figure 6-1 may look at bit overwhelming. However, after you start breaking down each process flow and subprocess, you and your staff will start finding pockets of misunderstanding, duplicate actions, and opportunities to be more efficient in your work flows.

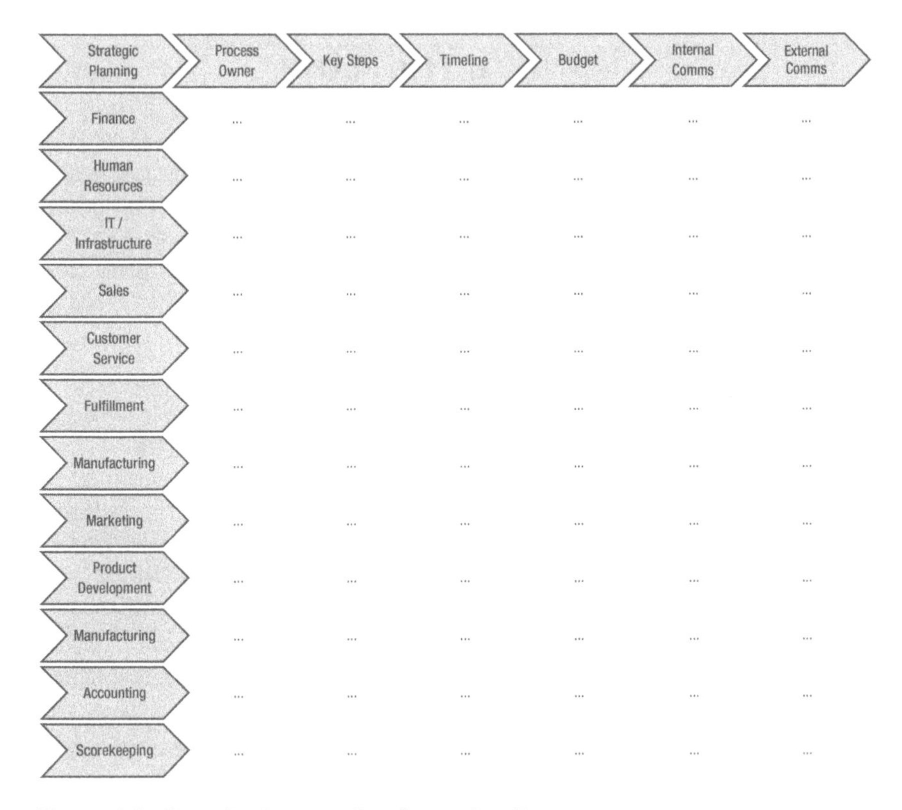

Figure 6-1. Example of process flow format for all processes

The first step is to identify critical process flows in your business. The areas listed on each row in the first column of Figure 6-1 should be most of the core process flows in your business. After you have chosen those appropriate for your business, assign owners to each of them. Note that it is quite common that a member of your team will be responsible for more than one process flow. It should also be noted that the CEO should not own every process flow. If he or she does, this is a sign of micro-managing and perhaps one of the bigger problems the company needs to overcome.

The ideal candidate to lead each process flow is someone who has a solid understanding of that function, who is well organized, and who gets along with his or her colleagues. Hopefully, these are your department heads. However, this may not necessarily be the case for some of your subprocess flows within a department.

GO WITH THE FLOW

A process flow does not have to be complicated for it to be effective. When I worked for CompuBank, NA, we set up a process flow for opening the mail and how the subsequent contents were to be handled by the back-office support team. One would think that opening the mail is a no-brainer. However, there were a lot of people in other departments that depended on the contents of the mail. Some of the mail was delivered directly to the office and some of it was sent to a Post Office (PO) box located in the building.

Hence, the first step was assigning someone to check the PO box on a daily basis so that the other critical steps would not be held up. The receptionists were assigned to notify the back office immediately when the mail carrier delivered the daily mail. When the mail was brought to the back room, the staff opened it and sorted the contents by category. Invoices went in one pile, to be given to accounting; checks from existing customers also went to accounting. Applications missing information and/or a signature were give to the marketing department's Customer Relationship Management (CRM) team to follow-up with each applicant, as were completed applications missing an initial deposit check or credit card number.

Feedback from the personnel reviewing the applications allowed us to improve the messaging in the application to reduce the rate of certain fields being missed by applicants. By setting up this process flow and communicating it internally, the back-office staff members not only understood better how their roles fit in with the bank's overall operations, but they also felt more appreciated by their colleagues in other departments who were depending on them.

A subset process flow takes specific areas of your departments and breaks them down by tasks. For example, your marketing department is responsible for all types of communications. However, the process flow for internal communications versus media communications versus customer communications versus investor communications are completely different, so you should map each subprocess accordingly. Assign a different person to lead each subprocess flow who is more involved with that specific subprocess than his or her colleagues. If you have only one person who manages all of marketing, it is even more important that this person document the process flow for each subarea. Otherwise, as mentioned, you put your company at risk of losing institutional memory if or when that person resigns or is laid off.

The next step for the process and subprocess owners is to lead a discussion to identify every key step in the process and to specify which colleagues are responsible for each step. It is important to note that the owners of each subprocess manage it, but they are not necessarily responsible for every step of the process because some tasks may be outside their area of expertise and even their department (such as finance, shipping, and so forth).

In addition, the owner of the process (or subprocess) may at times be managing staff members who are at a higher management level. However, this is irrelevant given the fact that *process flow trumps an organizational chart.* If a CEO is holding up a process flow because she has not signed off on a purchase order or signed a check that must be given to a supplier at the time of delivery, it is the role of the process owner to remind the CEO that she is holding up the process. This is equally true for colleagues in different departments. I hope you can see, from this example, that a process works only if there is consensus regarding the specific action items required by whom and in what time frame, at the outset of each process flow.

It is equally important to realize that if you have not already developed a process such as the one I just described, you are running the risk of operating your business at subpar performance. If, for example, the CEO and other department personnel already signed off on the process flow, they should accept a friendly nudge from the process owner to take the appropriate action that is holding up the company from operating at its optimal efficiency.

When you know who owns each process flow, and the key tasks are documented, it is important to develop for each task a timeline, metrics, and a budget. The first draft can be developed by each subprocess owner and then reviewed with the manager of the overall process. Start with the timeline. What is the frequency of each task? Is it daily, weekly, monthly, quarterly, or annually?

The next step is to develop the appropriate metrics for each process flow. Figure out by what measure you will rate whether the process flow is working well. For example, how many sales calls should a sales representative make in a day? What is the average amount of calls a customer service representative can take in an hour? How long should it take the truck drivers to make their daily deliveries to your stores? Develop some type of standard (set of metrics) against which to measure performance expectations, which will also affect resource budgeting.

Thereafter, develop a budget that contains both the human and financial resources required to implement all tasks in the process flow.

Document the Flow

After there is consensus on the process flow from all the parties involved directly with each process, the process owner must document the flow and determine how it is to be communicated to the rest of management and staff. Subprocess owners may require assistance from senior management as well from the head of internal communications (if there is someone designated for this role) to complete this step. By involving senior management during the documentation step, it will become readily apparent whether there are resource and/or scheduling conflicts with another process flow. What if two process flows have designated the use of a company resource (such as the company truck or the same personnel) at the same time? What if your chief financial officer says the company does not have the financial resources necessary to support the process flow the way it is designed?

In these instances, as well as others that inevitably arise, your team must improvise with the limited resources at their disposal. Remember, the key to determining and documenting the company's process flows is to figure out how your team can work as smart as possible given the resources available. Realistically, this is all that you can ask for.

Communicating the process flows effectively is important so that the various areas of the business understand how flows affect each area and interact with each area. In particular, the people responsible for specific tasks within one or several process flows need to be aware of how the flows work in sync with one another so they can budget their time effectively.

The final step in developing each process flow is communicating the flows externally. Senior management, process flow leaders, and the head of communications should determine which, if any, aspects of the respective process flows should be communicated outside the company. This step is important; appropriate expectations must be set with your customers, distributors, strategic partners, investors, and so on. For example, it is not adequate, regardless of the merits of the new policy, to change the store hours or hours of customer service support if the general public is not notified of the change via the company website, newsletter, signage on buildings, press releases, and so on. That said, the external communication team must determine the best medium to use to communicate each issue, whether it be customer service, investor relations, sales, advertising, and so forth.

It is important to note that working through each of the process flows is an iterative process. There is never a single best way to do every task in your company. By revisiting the process flows on a regular basis, you can tweak them to help you work smarter and more efficiently, which will help you on your way to turning your business around.

Note The value of mapping processes lies in your ability to make constant, incremental improvements with input from all of your staff. The flow is a working document; don't create one then stash it in a drawer.

Process Delineation Worksheet

There are no shortcuts to defining the key tasks in your process flows. After you identify owners for each of your process flows, give them a worksheet such as the one shown in Figure 6-2 (I've created this and used it successfully on behalf of my clients). The owners can either start to identify specific tasks for their process flow or gather a group of people from the relevant departments to brainstorm the process tasks. Competent process leaders also define the various tasks and indicate the employees responsible for each task. Thereafter, they share the flow to get consensus and buy-in from the appropriate process members.

Process Delineation Worksheet

Directions

Please use this worksheet to delineate individual steps of processes that you currently undertake in the normal course of your business day or week. Please use different sheets for distinctly different processes.

Find a quiet spot. Start with the middle column, and add steps of the process as they occur to you. Don't worry about writing down the steps in order from the beginning. Start with capturing what comes to mind first.

Either as you enter steps, or afterwards, in the third column add in the name of the person with whom you interface on that step.

After you have filled in both columns to your satisfaction, enter a number in the first column, corresponding with the order of the step in your process. These can be sorted afterward to put the steps of the process in their correct order.

Key ProcessTitle: ______________________________
(Select from any of the main process flows management had identified)

Sub-Process Title: ______________________________
(Please give this a descriptive name of your choosing; descriptions will be unified later)

Order	Process Step	Interface (Name)

Figure 6-2. Process delineation worksheet

If process leaders do not have a handle on the key tasks of a process flow, it is critical that they get input from the members of the appropriate departments. When meeting as a group to brainstorm the process tasks, process owners must be careful to delineate subprocess flows clearly. For example, your customer service reps may have one way of providing support to retail customers, another way for wholesale customers, and a third way for the sales representatives. Each of these three types of support may have different process flows, with different people in the customer service department responsible for them. These discussions can result in some confusion if subprocesses are not noted clearly. If this happens, consider this a win for that particular department and for the company as a whole. If there is confusion in a group brainstorming session, just think how these tasks must be playing out in reality on a daily basis. It is probably costing your firm a lot of wasted time and money, and a considerable amount of frustration as well. In a real-life situation, similar to the example presented here, a team unraveled some confusion and put in place a better a process flow solution that not only worked better for that department, but also helped increase customer satisfaction.

Example: Sales Process Flow

Figure 6-3 is an example of what a sales process flow might look like, with the various key tasks defined in detail, depending on the size of a particular company. The key point is how different employees from different departments have a role to play in the success of the sales process.

Process Delineation Worksheet

Key Process Title: Sales
(Select from any of the main process flows management had identified)

Sub-Process Title: ____________________
(Please give this a descriptive name of your choosing; descriptions will be unified later)

Order	Process Step	Interface (Name)
1	Identify Target Market	Product Development Manager or Market Research Manager
2	Develop Marketing Materials for Target Market to be used by Sales Representatives	Marketing Manager
3	Develop Advertising Campaign to Create Brand Awareness	Advertising Agency Rep or Marketing Manager
4	Create & Conduct Sales Product Overview Training	Product Manager
5	Create & Conduct Sales Training	Sales Manager or Sales Support Manager
6	Set Revenue Goals	CFO
7	Set lead generation, sales calls, meetings and revenue goals	Sales Manager
8	Execute Sales Goals	Each Individual Sales Rep
9	Track Performance Results	Each Sales Rep and/or Sales Support
10	Lead Weekly Sales Meetings	Sales Manager

Figure 6-3. Sales process delineation worksheet

In Figure 6-3, step 1 in the process is to identify the target market for the products or services being offered. Identifying the market is, in this case, probably a joint effort between the product development manager and marketing or market research manager, in conjunction with the sales manager. Let's take a look at how the steps interact.

Step 1: The results of this step (identify the target market) should be reported in detail to the marketing manager who is in charge of....

Step 2: Here you develop marketing materials for the target market to be used by sales representatives. It is absolutely critical that the marketing manager know who the product manager thinks is going to be buying the company's products and services so that he or she can create the most effective marketing materials possible. Leaving it up to the marketing manager to guess is not a formula for success.

Step 3: This step is synergistic with step 2. Although some firms create their brochures and marketing materials in-house, they still might outsource their advertising campaign to an advertising agency. It is important, therefore, that the advertising agency account rep be a part of the process flow planning. The more the agency knows about the target market and the materials that have already been developed in-house by the marketing manager, the more synergistic the advertising is going to be. In addition, because ad agencies usually handle the media buy on behalf of their client, it is important that the account rep inform the sales process team of the flight schedule for the media buy. In this example, I am also presuming that the marketing manager was already given a budget in the marketing process flow by the chief financial officer.

Step 4: This step consists of creating and conducting sales product overview training led by the product manager. No one knows the feature benefits of the product and/or service better than the person in charge of developing it.

Step 5: This step, creating and conducting sales training, should be led by the sales manager, who should know more about how to close the deal with the target audience better than anyone.

Step 6: Revenue goals should be determined by the chief financial officer, who is in charge of the overall budget for the entire company.

Step 7: This step is about setting lead generation, sales calls, meetings, and individual sales rep revenue goals. It should be handled by the sales manager.

Step 8: Executing sales goals is managed by each individual sales rep.

Step 9: Tracking performance results should be managed by each sales rep and/or by the sales support manager, if your company is big enough to have one.

Step 10: This step, leading weekly sales meetings, should be managed by the sales manager because he or she is ultimately in charge of motivating, managing, and holding the sales team accountable for reaching the stated revenue goals.

It is important to note that five of these ten steps are managed by professionals who are not part of the sales team. They are, however, an integral part of the sales process flow. Thus, it is essential that there be excellent cross-departmental collaboration to achieve improved operational efficiencies.

Note Most process flows require collaboration with people in other departments who perform other functions. Staying on good terms with people in all parts of the company is an important point to make to your team.

After you have consensus on the various steps to each process flow, put them into a flowchart and table as shown in Figure 6-4. These documents should become your playbook/operational manual for your company. It is a constant work-in-progress and a critical planning tool.

	Identify Target Market	Develop Marketing Materials	Develop Ad Campaign	Create and Conduct Product Training	Create and Conduct Sales Training
Owner	product development manager or market research manager	marketing manager	advertising agency rep or marketing manager	product manager	sales manager or sales support manager
Timeline	during product development process	prior to product being launched	depends in part on budget and the seasonality of the products/ services	before ad campaign launches	before ad campaign launches and ongoing
Key Metrics	size of market	should be printed as needed	audience reach	level of sales reps confidence	sales results
Budget	determined by CFO	determined by CFO	determined by marketing manager	determined by marketing manager	determined by sales manager
Internal Communications	FAQs on company Intranet	should be noted where they can be found	flight schedule should be posted on Intranet and discussed in meetings	training materials schedule should be posted on Intranet	training materials schedule should be posted on Intranet
External Communications	na	na	potential press release and social media push	na	na

	Set Revenue Goals	Set Individual Goals	Execute Sales Goals	Track Performance Results	Lead Weekly Sales Meetings
Owner	CFO	sales manager	each individual rep	each individual rep and/or sales support	sales manager
Timeline	quarterly	quarterly	weekly	weekly	weekly
Key Metrics	actual vs. goal	actual vs. goal	actual vs. goal	actual vs. goal	actual vs. goal
Budget	determined by CFO	determined by sales manager	determined by sales manager	determined by sales manager	determined by sales manager
Internal Communications	you may want only sales reps to have access to this info	you may want only sales reps to have access to this info	you may want only sales reps to have access to this info	you may want only sales reps to have access to this info	you may want only sales reps to have access to this info
External Communications	na	na	na	na	na

Figure 6-4. Sample sales process flow

When you and your staff look at the final draft of your own sales process flow, as well as other process flows in this format, you should be much more confident that the left hand in your firm knows what the right hand is doing and vice versa. This is not an easy exercise to conduct. However, it is a critical one to undertake for your company to maximize its output with the least amount of time, human, and financial resources.

Example of a Subprocess Flow

You may find that, after getting consensus on the functional process flow—in this case, the sales process flow—you and your staff are ready to drill down even farther to subprocess flows. The more specific the tasks to a process are defined, the better everyone on your staff will understand exactly what they are responsible for and with whom they should be interacting. The following example (Figure 6-5) is of a sales subprocess flow that focuses on step 10 of the sales process—leading weekly sales meetings.

Process Delineation Worksheet

Key Process Title: Sales
(Select from any of the main process flows management had identified)

Sub-Process Title: Weekly Sales Meetings
(Please give this a descriptive name of your choosing; descriptions will be unified later)

Order	Process Step	Interface (Name)
1	Confirm Date & Meeting Time or Dial In Number	Sales Support Manager or Administrative Assistant
2	Review Weekly, Monthly, Quarterly and Annual Sales Goals	Sales Manager
3	Review Individual Sales Reps and Team Weekly Performance (e.g. calls, meetings and sales – actual vs. plan)	Sales Support or Sales Manager
4	Review customer feedback, challenges and successes	Sales Reps
5	Review Media Flight Schedule for Next Week	Marketing Manager

Figure 6-5. Weekly sales meeting subprocess flow: delineated tasks

> **Step 1:** Confirm the date, time, and location or dial-in number of the meeting. This task should be executed by the sales support manager or an administrative assistant.
>
> **Step 2:** Review the weekly, monthly, quarterly, and annual sales goals.

Step 3: Review individual sales reps and team weekly performance (such as calls, meetings, and sales—actual vs. the plan). This task should be led by either the sales manager or sales support manager.

Step 4: Review customer feedback, challenges, and successes. This task should be led by the manager of the sales reps.

Step 5: Review the media flight schedule for next week. If there is one, it should be reviewed by the marketing manager.

Just like the higher level sales process flow, it is important to garner consensus on the various tasks associated with each subprocess flow. Thereafter, put them in a flowchart and table, as shown in Figure 6-6.

	Confirm Meeting (Date, Time, Dial-In Numbers)	Review Weekly, Monthly, Quartely, Annual Sales Goals	Review Individuals Reps' Performances (Actual vs. Plan)	Review Customer Feedback, Challenges, and Sucesses	Review Upcoming Media Flight Schedule
Owner	sales support manager or administrative assistant	sales manager	sales support or sales manager	sales reps	marketing manager
Timeline	week in advance	weekly	weekly	weekly	week prior to media campaign
Key Metrics	attendance	actual vs. plan	actual vs. plan	is feedback improving over time	scope of media buy
Budget	determined by sales manager	na	na	na	na
Internal Communications	should be posted on company calendar	access should be for sales reps only	access should be for sales reps only	feedback should be company intranet for customer service and product development	flight schedule should be posted on intranet for customer service and media relations
External Communications	na	na	na	may impact the company's messaging	na - this is covered in the sales process flow

Figure 6-6. Weekly sales meeting subprocess flow: flowchart and table

The more you and your team get into this exercise for each of your process flows and subsequent subprocess flows, the easier the exercise gets. Pretty soon, you will start to hear some of your staff asking insightful questions in staff meetings regarding the impact that a proposed project will have on another department's resource constraints and vice versa. When this happens, note that you're creating a company culture that encourages your staff members to think before they act, which improves your company's operational efficiency greatly and, ultimately, its profitability.

Create a binder that contains all the key process flows and subprocess flows. You may even want copies made for senior management. Each department head and staff member should have copies of their respective process flows and subprocess flows, which should be reviewed in planning meetings and refined as the group believes appropriate. Make sure all your process flows are dated so that there is no version confusion when they are updated.

Note As the idea of process flows seeps into your company culture, you'll be amazed at the insights that bubble up from your employees. They will suggest real improvements and start to think before they act, putting your company on the path to a successful turnaround.

Summary

Managing your overall operational process flow better may be a new concept for you and your management team. Initially, it may be an uncomfortable process for a company that has been personality driven. Developing a process flow will help your staff members determine how they should assign and execute responsibilities as well as how they should collaborate with their colleagues.

The first step in this exercise is to identify the critical process flows of your business, then assign someone to be responsible for each flow. Thereafter, the process owner should lead a discussion with appropriate staff to determine the key tasks in implementing the process flow successfully.

Sometimes, having your team fill out a form to outline their understanding of the key steps is an effective way to delineate the process flow. Don't be surprised if there is some initial confusion about who does what when and with whom. In addition, subprocess flows may stem from these discussions. Subprocess flows are developed in the same manner as the larger process flows. After the tasks have been identified, determine the timeline/frequency of these tasks, key metrics, relevant budget issues, and what (if any) internal and external communications need to occur. Mapping the process flow in a graphic visual with an associated table that depicts the specifics of the process or subprocess is a great framework for managing your company's operations. Remember, defining process flows is an iterative task that is essential to strategic planning.

PART

III

Increasing Marketing and Sales Efficiency

CHAPTER

7

How to Understand Your Customers, Competitors, and Key Trends Better

Getting Realigned with the Market

It is quite understandable that when an entrepreneur is in what appears to be an endless cycle of simultaneous cash flow problems and operations battles, it is easy to get out of touch with customers, with what competitors are doing, and with the various shifts in key industry trends.

Nonetheless, it is critical that you get realigned with market realities before you make any kind of major sales and marketing push.

This chapter's objective is to help you come up with some simple but pragmatic approaches to getting a better handle on your market and its drivers so that you can plan more effective sales and marketing campaigns. These tasks are going to take some discipline and faith in the process, because this exercise is not an immediate cost-saving or cash-generating undertaking such as the recommendations made in Chapters 2 and 3 regarding managing accounts payables and accounts receivables better. However, the suggestions proposed in this chapter will no doubt either save you money and/or help you make money after you are back on offense. The simple fact of the matter is that the more aligned your sales and marketing efforts are with market realities—rather than with outdated assumptions—the better your results will be.

Know Your Customers as Well as, If Not Better Than, Your Products and Services

I am always amazed how my clients talk about their products with such pride—like they were their kids—but how little they know about their customers. If you have a consumer business, the name of the game in the digital era is to be primarily consumer focused rather than product or service focused. The reason for this new reality is that, with the Internet, social media, and a plethora of private databases, you have an abundance of information about your customers today that did not exist a generation ago. Even if you are a business-to-business company, you have a number of ways to get feedback from your customers. In addition, with all the advances in manufacturing and global competition, product cycles in many sectors are becoming shorter and shorter. What is hot this year may be out of style next year for a whole host of reasons over which you have no control. However, you do have control over how much you know about, treat, and communicate with your customers. Never ever take your customers for granted.

Tip If declining sales and poor operational execution haven't helped you realize it already, take note now: Never, ever take customers for granted. They are your life's blood.

Segment Your Customer Base

It is critical that you segment your customer base to help you prioritize your sales and marketing efforts. Break down your customer base into subgroups based on revenue levels and types of customers based on behavior, gender, geography, income, and so forth. Although all customers should be treated with equal respect, they may not be entitled to the same level of service based on what they are purchasing. Nor should your sales and marketing efforts be allocated equally toward acquiring different types of customers. Some customer types are easier to acquire, and therefore cost less per acquisition. Other customers tend to purchase high-margin products, but they may cost more to acquire than other customer types. Acquiring this information is not as hard as you might expect, but it does take a concerted effort to amass it.

Here's an example of segmenting a customer base. An online publishing web site may have an easier time getting some viewers to give their contact information and e-mail for access to some content, but they can only convert a small portion of that customer base to pay for greater access to more content. I would classify the free users as interested (for example, they did take the time to give you their name, address, and e-mail), but infrequent and/or low-budget users. They are, nonetheless, still important to the online business, because the traffic they produce is important for generating advertising revenues. The user who is willing to pay is either a high-income user that isn't concerned about the fee or a frequent user that wants to have regular, full access to the content. These two customer segments may have different needs and require a different approach from the online publisher to keeping them engaged.

There are a number of ways, depending on their respective relevancy, of how to segment your existing client base to understand your customers more fully. To segment your customer base, answer the following questions:

- What is the demographic profile of your customer base?
- What is the geographic profile?
- What is the psychographic profile?
- How do they differ in terms of sales volume (aka revenue breakdown)?

Break down your answers to each of these questions by percentages so that you get a more precise picture of your customers.

Demographic Profile

Knowing the demographic profile is especially important if you are in a consumer-oriented business, because you can make more precise judgments on your packaging, pricing, and promotion of your products and services. Here are a few questions to ask:

- Are your customers male or female?
- Are they the user of your products and services or the gatekeepers (for example, are they purchasing for their kids, elderly parents, spouse, and so on)?
- What is the age range of your customers?
- What is the ethnicity of your customers?
- What is the income of your customers?

Knowing the answers to these questions will help you develop a more effective marketing strategy. For example, I had a client whose biggest customer base was women, but the majority of the company's advertising was aimed at men, which was clearly an inefficient use of precious marketing resources. The same goes for having an understanding of who is purchasing the product versus who is actually using the product. A perfect example of this is on Mother's Day or Father's Day. Mothers or fathers are not likely going to purchase a gift for themselves on these holidays. Hence, an advertiser is walking a fine line of appealing to a family gatekeeper (such as the spouse or adult children) to make a purchase they think their parent or spouse is going to like. Is your marketing appealing to just one audience or two? In addition, knowing the age, race, ethnicity, and income of your customer base can provide unique insights into more effective messaging, because these variables are somewhat correlated in many markets.

Geographic Profile

Knowing where your customers live and/or work is important for understanding a number of issues. If you have a restaurant or retail store, you want to know where your customers live and/or work so you have a better idea of where to advertise. Your advertising assumptions may not match reality. If you are advertising in a neighborhood paper but your customers are coming from across town or from the office buildings in your area, you are wasting money. Knowing where your customers live can also be a way of determining income, ethnicity, and age. The U.S. Census (`www.census.gov`) allows you to look up zip codes and determine ethnic, age, and income breakdowns in a matter of minutes. This information is especially important to know if you have a consumer online business, because you don't get to see your customers or the cars they drive. Thus, short of asking them, the address they give when making a purchase is the only variable you have to work with to get a better understanding of who they are.

Tip Knowing where your customers live can also tell you a lot about their demographic characteristics, including ethnicity and income.

Psychographic Profile

A psychographic profile is a profile based on behavioral characteristics rather than traditional demographics such as age, gender, and race. I often work with clients who think they know their clients really well. However, I throw them for a loop when I ask them to describe five types of customers without telling me anything about their demographic or geographic profile. They have been so focused on developing their product and services they have not spent enough time thinking about the *behavior* of their clients. This knowledge is important, because if you understand the needs and desires of your clients, you can do a better job of deciding which products and services to sell to meet those needs and desires.

Wikipedia cites the technology adoption life cycle illustrated in Figure 7-1 as a sociological model developed by John N. Bohlen, George M. Beal, and Everett M. Rogers at Iowa State University, and built on earlier research conducted by Neal C. Gross and Bryce Ry. This bell curve helps marketers profile customer segments to determine pricing, promotion, and placement of products and services.

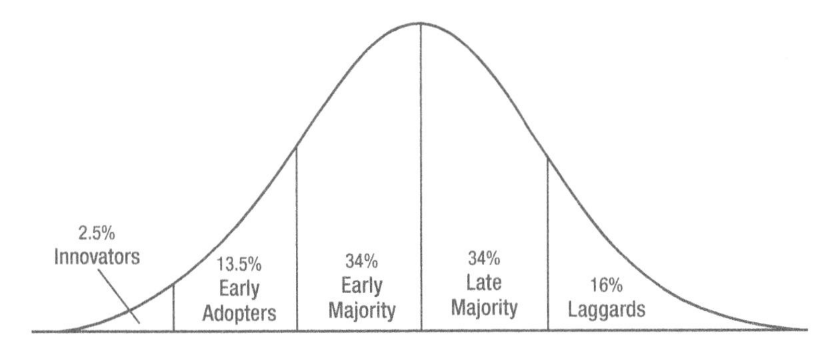

Figure 7-1. Bell curve adoption profile

Each segment of the bell curve has different characteristics, depending on the market. Describe your customer attributes in each of these segments.

The bell curve is often used to explain consumer behavior with high-technology products. An innovator may be a gadget geek that is always looking toward the future with technological innovations. This person may have a device (such as a three-dimensional printer) way before most people even think about it. An early adopter might be someone in your neighborhood, office, or family who is always the first person to have the latest Apple device, even if he or she paid a premium for it. Consumers in the early majority might have disposable income and see technology as a way of getting ahead, whether for themselves or for their kids. The late majority sees the advantage of the technology but is going to wait until the price drops enough to where it becomes affordable. A laggard is someone who is holding out on purchasing or using a piece of technology that is now mainstream. Someone who does not use e-mail, a cell phone, or social media may be considered a laggard from a market segmentation perspective. The most important aspect to take away from the defining of these various segments is for you to know into which segment your core customer base falls so that you have a better understanding of your customers' behavior.

You may have a mature product offering, such as food or hardware, for which the bell curve is not an appropriate tool to segment your customers. If so, use these types of customer profiles:

- Customers will pay a premium for service because they have limited time.
- Customers will drive across town for a sale because they like to save money.
- Customers like to shop at night.
- Customers like to shop online at work for convenience.
- Customers like to shop online at night after a long day.
- Customers like to do research before making a purchase.
- Customers like to walk in and talk to a salesperson.

- Customers like to talk to a person via customer service over the telephone or via a chat box online.
- Customers want to make a purchase without having to talk with anyone.

The point in listing all these examples is for you and your team to come up with a set of psychographics for your business and then to segment your customer base into each of the profiles. By segmenting your customers into a psychographic profile, you have a much broader understanding of your customer base. Thereafter, you can back into the demographic and geographic profiles of your customer base to prepare an effective marketing strategy.

Figure 7-2 is an example of a psychographic segmentation of a consumer base. By creating such a framework, it allows a marketing team to understand more completely the idiosyncratic behavior of its customer base. Thereafter, the marketing team can identify its target customer segments, in part by ranking them. Then, the team can match a demographic segmentation, as shown in Figure 7-3, to the psychographic segmentation to identify and target its ideal customer segments more successfully.

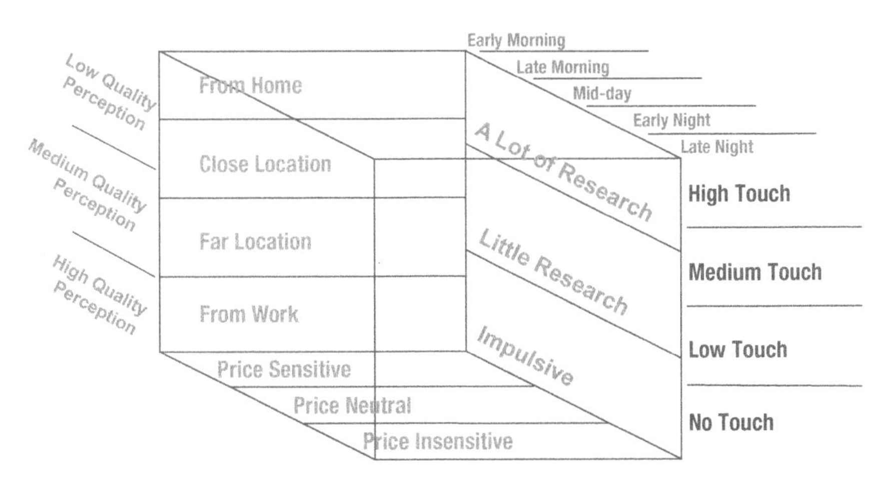

Figure 7-2. Psychographic segmentation

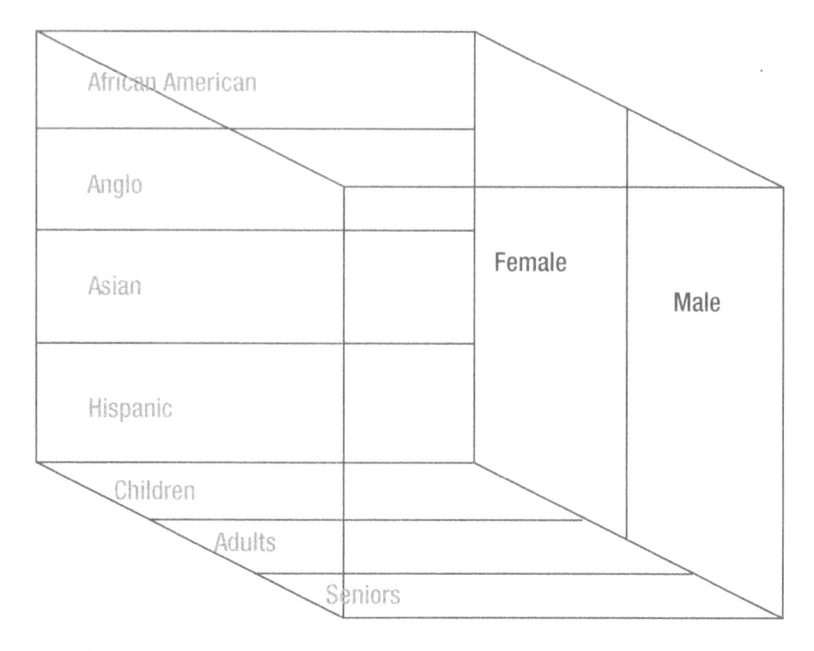

Figure 7-3. Demographic segmentation

Revenue Breakdown

One way in which many companies segment and then rank their customer base is by revenue breakdown.

- What is the average total ticket purchase per customer? Some point-of-sales systems generate this information in a simple report. If yours does not, divide the total number of transactions by the total revenue to get the average ticket purchase. Ideally, you would plot the various purchases by price points so that you can throw out the extreme highs and extreme lows to get a better sense of the average ticket price for most of your customers.
- What is the average number of items purchased?
- What is the average price per item purchased?

For the sake of simplicity, try dividing the answers to each of the previous questions into four segments. The first two segments should be in some defined ranged of acceptance below and above the average. The second two segments will be outside these defined ranges—below and above the average. Depending on what the results look like, you can even bifurcate into eight segments, and so on, until you feel like you can make a real distinction in your various types of customers just by breakdown purchases by revenue amount.

Review and analyze the results of your psychographic, demographic, geographic, and revenue breakdown findings to get a much clearer profile of your customers and to segment them further into the subclasses great customers, good customers, and customers you don't want. Remember, all customers deserve equal respect, but they don't merit equal focus. It is critical that you focus your primary sales and marketing resources on those customer segments that make you the most money, and that you quit spending money on customers that cost you money.

If this is still confusing, pick a profit margin range you want to make (such as 25% to 30%). You may have customer segments that are actually producing a 30% to 35% profit margin, some that are producing 25% to 30%, some that are producing 5% to 10%, and some that are actually losing money. In this example, the segment that is producing 25% to 30% should be your primary target segment. If you cannot fix quickly the problem with the segment that is losing money, discontinue it as soon as possible. The other segments should be ranked primarily by the amount of margin they are producing.

Use Customer Surveys to Help Fill in the Gaps

Ironically, you may have more questions about your customer base after going through the previous exercise than you had before doing it. The simplest and best way to get consumer feedback is a survey. (For business customers, the survey can be conducted in person by your sales reps.) It does not matter whether the survey is sent via e-mail, mailed, or conducted over the phone. The point is to get some candid and constructive feedback as soon as possible. Conduct a customer survey at least twice a year until your company is back on track. The survey serves as another metric to determine whether your customers are noticing the improvements you are making. The following is an example of a simple customer survey.

EXAMPLE OF CUSTOMER SURVEY

June 1, 2014

Dear Customer,

I want to thank you for your business. In order for our company to meet your needs more fully, we are conducting a brief customer survey. I would appreciate your candid feedback.

Thank You!

Jon Doe
President

On a scale of 1 to 10 (with 10 being the highest) please rate the following:

How satisfied are you with our company's products and services? ____

How would you rate our sales and customer service team? ____

How likely are you to continue doing business with us? ____

How likely are you to recommend our products and services to others? ____

From which other companies do you purchase the same products and services?

____

What are three improvements our company can make?

1. ____

2. ____

3. ____

Learn from Your Competitors

In most of the companies with which I have worked, competitor actions create very few business-crippling problems. This is why I have waited until the seventh chapter of this book to discuss your competitors. You need to focus on cleaning up internal problems before you spend any time worrying about your competitors. Nonetheless, there is much benefit to be gained by learning from your competitors, especially before you develop a sales and marketing strategy. Furthermore, you can be assured that your savvy competitors are certainly trying to learn as much as they can from your business. In fact, they may be dealing with many of the same problems your firm is facing. If your competitors are handling similar problems more effectively than you, it is in your best interest to gain as much insight from them as possible.

Note Although it is easy to point to your competitors as the source of your troubles, they rarely are. Usually, business problems are self-made.

Identify Your Competitors

It is important to develop a list of your competitors to track their activity periodically. Don't get fooled into thinking that you do not have competitors. Of course you do. Every business has competitors, whether they are direct competitors or competitors for "wallet share." In addition, every company that does what your business does is not a direct competitor. If your customers have never heard of a particular company that does what your firm does, and that firm's customers' have never heard of your firm, you are not really competing with one another.

Start your list with the companies that your customers noted in the customer survey—in other words, those businesses from which they purchase the same products and services. You want a better understanding of why your customer is using these companies and not your company. If your list is less than three companies long, segment the companies you perceive to be your competitors by ranking them on the basis of who is competing for your primary customer segments.

Figure 7-4 illustrates a way of segmenting your competitors based on the psychographic segmentation in Figure 7-2. This example is from the perspective of a small-neighborhood convenience and grocery store. At first glimpse, it would appear that all these companies are competitors to the small-neighborhood convenience store. However, I argue that not all of them are competitors. How the owner of the store ranks her own customers, based on the psychographic segmentation, determines which companies listed are primary competitors, secondary competitors, and perhaps no concern at all.

Potential Competitors to a Small-Neighborhood Convenience Store	
High Quality Perception	Local Farmer's Market
Medium Quality Perception	SafeWay
Low Quality Perception	Walmart
High Cost	Gas Station
Medium Cost	Local Drug Store
Low Cost	Walmart
From Home	NA
Close Location	SafeWay
Far Location	Walmart
From Work	NA
Impulsive	NA
Little Research	NA
A Lot of Research	NA
Early Morning	CVS
Late Morning	Gas Station, Local Drug Store, Walmart
Midday	Gas Station, Local Drug Store, Walmart
Early Night	Gas Station, Local Drug Store, Walmart
Late Night	CVS
No Touch	CVS
Low Touch	Walmart
Medium Touch	SafeWay
High Touch	Local Farmer's Market

Figure 7-4. Competitive segmentation

Review Competitors' Web Sites and Social Media

The first step in learning about your competitors' product offerings, pricing, promotion, and positioning strategies is to review each of their respective web sites, Facebook pages, Twitter accounts, LinkedIn and Flicker sites, and so on. While conducting this review, pay particular attention to what your competitors emphasize. Are they product- and service-centric or price driven? Is their message consistent across all the social media platforms or are they all over the map? Do they list their prices? If so, how do they compare with yours? What do they do better than your business? What can you learn from them and incorporate to help your business? What does your business do better than each of your competitors? Is there a consistent theme on your strengths and weaknesses vis-à-vis the collective group of competitors? Does their messaging target specific psychographic profiles?

Find your competitors' advertising campaigns—online, print, radio, and/or TV—to help you determine the consistency and effectiveness of their promotional efforts. If they are consistent in their messaging, you can be assured they are good at planning. If their messaging is inconsistent, you can be pretty confident their efforts are not very effective.

You can determine the demographic your competitors are targeting, in part by where they advertise. Do they advertise in an ethnic paper? In which section of the mainstream paper do they buy advertising space? On which TV channels do they advertise? What time of the day do they advertise? The answers to all these questions will help you define your competitors' target customer better.

When I was running the marketing department for CompuBank, NA, the first virtual national bank, I conducted a competitive assessment of our competitors, all of which were large, national traditional banks that were introducing online banking to their customer base. What I quickly realized, based on reviewing their web sites and advertising campaigns, was that they were spending big bucks on traditional media to promote their online banking, but their online presence, including their own web site, was weak. Given the fact that CompuBank, NA, was a small startup bank with limited marketing funds, I decided to put almost all our marketing resources into online marketing. As an Internet-only bank, our marketing team was much more Internet savvy than our competitors, in part because they had no traditional marketing responsibilities given our business model. If our marketing team had not done a thorough review of these larger banks, we would have assumed these banks knew what they were doing online and we may have had more traditional marketing (such as TV, radio, and print) in our mix. As a result of these factors, as well as our bank's ease of use, CompuBank was rated the number one bank online by *Smart Money* magazine's third annual survey of online banks in 1999.

Google Your Competitors

It is amazing what you can find out about your competitors just by looking them up on Google. You can find press releases they have issued, articles written about them, as well as customer postings on various consumer-oriented blogs. All this information, along with the information found on their respective web sites and via social media, should give you a better picture of your competitors' activities. This knowledge should help you position your company better to play up your strengths and their weaknesses. You'll also be in a better position to mitigate your weaknesses.

Check out Competitors at Trade Shows

Trade shows are another venue for finding out more information about your competitors. Looking at your competitors' trade show booths can reveal other information regarding how they position themselves in the marketplace. Trade shows also offer an opportunity to pick up your competitors brochures. In addition, you can get a feel for how aggressive they are in the marketplace by noting how many people they have working their booth and whether they are hosting any trade show events.

Tip Trade shows are excellent places to gather business intelligence. Visiting a competitor's booth should yield a lot of information you can put to use in developing or revamping your strategies.

Size Your Competitors

Do you know how big your competitors are? There are a number of private database services in the marketplace (such as Dun & Bradstreet, Equifax, InfoUSA, and so forth) that provide reports, albeit outdated and not totally accurate, about them. These reports can give you a baseline estimate on the number of employees they have as well as their annual revenue. Knowing how many locations a retail competitor has can be a good way to estimate its annual revenue, especially if you assume its cost structure is similar to that of your firm's. In addition, knowing if they are a subsidiary of a larger company will give you an idea of their ability to access capital.

Pay Attention to Industry and Macro Trends

It is important to have a solid understanding of the key drivers in your industry so that you know whether your industry is projected to grow, remain steady, or decline during the next three to five years. Are your industry's analysts and experts predicting major structural changes in your industry (such as health care) or are they predicting limited structural change (such as commodity type products - coal, sugar, or salt)? Will there be more or fewer government regulations related to your industry? Will there be new competitors entering the industry or are your competitors leaving the industry?

Join an industry trade association to access key industry trends and acquire answers to many of the questions listed in the previous paragraph. In addition, you'll have access to trade association staff members, who spend a lot of their time talking to companies in your region and across the country that are similar to yours. Often, when a company is having cash flow challenges, management cancels its trade association membership. This is especially true if managers are not taking advantage of the services to which membership entitles them, such as attending the association's annual trade show and conference as well as networking with other similar businesses from different parts of the country that may be experiencing the same types of challenges your firm is facing. Maintain or reinstate your trade association membership, especially if you have not been active in it for a period of time. Going to a trade show can reinvigorate you, get you up to date on what your competitors are doing, and expose you to out-of-the-box thinking as well as the latest trends presented by experts in your field.

I am often engaged by clients to help size their market and to identify key market trends. Whenever I work in a specialized market (such as manufacturing, specialized health care, and so on) where industry data are not readily available on the Internet, I make contact immediately with the research department of that sector's trade associations. I am very candid about the type of information I am seeking. At a minimum, I get some insightful guidance regarding where I can find this data via other organizations of which I have no previous knowledge. In many instances, the association has a study for sale—discounted to members—that can answer many of the questions for which I am seeking the answers.

Understand Macro Trends That Drive Your Industry

Although it is important to stay current on industry trends, it is equally important to understand how the broader economy impacts your sector. Some companies do well in recessions because they sell an "affordable" luxury that customers are purchasing in hard times, in part because they have stopped spending money on what they perceive to be more luxurious products and services. Other companies take a direct hit to their sales when the economy is in trouble. If you were in the travel business in 2008, you probably experienced a major decrease in sales, as did the residential real estate market. However, Starbucks' sales actually increased during that time period. They key is to understand what drives your customers' decision-making process and the macro trends that impact their decisions.

I was hired as an interim president of a 40-year-old retail and wholesale sandwich business that was in need of turning around. The business sold "po-boys," a submarine-type sandwich originating from Louisiana. The owner wanted to improve the quality of his products, which were at one time well known and well liked around its region of operation. In his attempt to improve the quality of the ingredients, he wanted to change the nature of the po-boy sandwiches, as well as the price point, so it was more like a high-end deli sandwich one would purchase at a New York–style delicatessen. Although I supported his efforts to improve the quality of the product, I argued with him that changing the pricing of the po-boy sandwiches would hurt sales, given the nature of his clientele and the reputation of his brand.

I am the type of consultant that tells my clients what I think they need to hear, not what they want to hear. Otherwise, I lose my credibility. When I realized I was not doing an effective job of communicating my point, I reminded him these types of sandwiches were perceived to be first created during the Great Depression; thus, there was a reason why they were called po-boys. I further argued that, by changing the nature of the sandwich and its pricing, he would only—at best—be satisfying rich boys. I am certainly not opposed to doing business with clients that have expensive taste; however, that particular business was built on the masses and not on a sliver of the population. My final argument was so compelling that there was no rational reason he could argue with it. Although he did improve the quality of the sandwiches' ingredients, which I supported, he did not change the volume of ingredients or the affordable price points. As a result, he was able to increase his sales in grocery stores.

Tip Stay abreast of the national and global economy. Regardless of the business you're in, it will affect you and the decisions you make.

Summary

The goal of this chapter was to get you realigned with three critical elements in every business: your customers, your competitors, and key trends in your sector. Each should be part of the basis of your sales and marketing strategy. You must also be up to date on each of these elements before you spend a penny on your sales and marketing efforts; otherwise, you may be throwing your money away.

Understanding, segmenting, and ranking your customers is a must if you want to be more effective at retaining the ones you want to keep, knowing which ones you should not go after, and attracting new customer—as cost-effectively as possible. Reviewing and analyzing the information you already collected on your customers is the first step in the process. Conducting customer surveys is a good and inexpensive tool to use to get to know your customers better.

Identifying and learning from your competitors is another critical element in the planning of your sales and marketing strategies. Acknowledge the fact that every company has competitors, even if it don't think it does. In addition, understand that not every company that does the same thing as yours is necessarily a competitor. You can learn a lot about your competitors from reviewing their web and social media sites as well as by Googling them. You can learn a lot about your competitors at trade shows as well as by purchasing reports from private database companies.

Having an updated understanding of industry trends and the macro trends that impact your business is also critical to your sales and marketing planning. To help you plan for the future, know whether your industry is growing, its regulation trends, its competitive trends, and the macro economic trends that impact your business.

Last, if you use the findings from your customer, competitor, and industry trend analyses while developing of your sales and marketing strategies, it is virtually impossible not to make more prudent business decisions in your planning than you have in the past, when you did not use them.

CHAPTER

8

How to Develop a More Effective Marketing Strategy

Consistency Gets You Faster Success

This chapter's objective is to help you conduct a marketing gap assessment so you become more aware of where you can be more effective with your marketing efforts. This may be a frustrating, but enlightening, process for you. If you can be objective and step out of the framework in which you have been thinking about marketing, you are going to see that your firm has probably wasted a lot of marketing dollars, because your marketing team, and advertising and public relations agencies, are probably focused more on tactics than strategy.

I have had the privilege of being trained by some of the best marketing professionals in the world at the Wharton School, all of whom approach marketing in a strategic manner. Hence, I am somewhat biased in my approach to marketing and have helped a lot of companies with their marketing efforts during the past 20 years. I am convinced that most outside marketing and ad agencies mean well, but they have an inherent conflict of interest with their clients because of the way they get paid. Simply put, ad agencies get paid a percentage of what you spend on your advertising. Therefore, they are never going to tell you not to advertise. In addition, how effective can their campaigns be if they are not privy to knowing your product margins (which you may not even know) or have an understanding of your existing customers, competitors, and marketing trends?

You may recall that, back in Chapter 1, I recommended that you stop spending money on your marketing efforts. I made the assumption that your marketing efforts have been ineffective, given the situation your company is facing. Until you know your margins on your products and, as discussed in Chapter 7, your preferred target customer segmentation, your competitors, and current market trends, you should not spend money on marketing. You need to preserve your cash flow. I am confident that this will make more sense to you after reading this chapter. If it still does not make sense, I suggest you review the chapter with a close business associate to garner his or her perspective on what is being recommended.

Tip I can't say it often enough: *Stop spending money on marketing* until you have done an assessment and have a sound strategy in place.

It Should Be "Marketing and Sales," *Not* "Sales and Marketing"

I know it is easier verbally to say "sales and marketing" than it is to say "marketing and sales." However, you have to have a good marketing plan before you can develop an effective sales plan; otherwise, you are not maximizing your potential for success. A good marketing plan allows your sales team to have faster success or faster failure. Having faster success is a no-brainer, but why would anyone want faster failure? The answer is simple. The faster you know that the market is not responding to your marketing and sales efforts, the better chance you have of finding out why and then making the necessary adjustments.

What's more, marketing and sales people should get paid for results. The only way to get results is to make mistakes, learn from them as quickly as possible, and repeat the cycle as quickly and cost-effectively as possible. When the cost per customer acquisition goes up instead of down, or it levels out, you know the marketing team is running out of its ideal customer segment. Or, it is targeting the next-tier segment, which may be more expensive to acquire. Or, as is the case for most businesses that don't review analytics, it is not learning and ends up panic buying by just throwing money into marketing as if it was putting money down on the roulette table in a casino. All great marketers make mistakes, but not the same one for very long, because they analyze every data point they can access to maximize where they can get the biggest bang for the marketing buck. It should be noted that analytics don't have to be complicated, but they do have to be consistent; otherwise, they provide limited value. Back in Chapter 6, I encouraged you to document each step of your major process flows, determine the appropriate metrics to track, and then to review these metrics on an ongoing basis. When a marketing department does not document processes and track metrics, it is not learning and thus is vulnerable of wasting precious working capital.

Note You need a good marketing plan before you can develop a good sales plan.

What Is Marketing?

Professor Phillip Kotler, Johnson and Son Distinguished Professor of International Marketing at the Kellogg School of Management at Northwestern University and author of numerous marketing books, defines marketing as "not the art of finding clever ways to dispose of what you make. It is the art of creating genuine customer value." I find this quote especially relevant living in the digital age in which there is so much information about a company's customers that can be accessed easily, as well as so many ways to stay in touch with a company's customers. In the predigital age, it was difficult and expensive to know a lot about a customer base as well to stay in regular contact; hence, a company had to be primarily product or service oriented.

The digital age is in constant evolution, with a major breakthrough every decade if not sooner. The personal computer was developed during the early 1980s. The browser was developed during the early-to-mid 1990s. The acceptance of smartphones began during the 2000s. Since 2010, social media has exploded. Regardless of the amazing technological innovations that have been developed, I find that most companies still approach their marketing efforts based on the predigital paradigm represented in Figure 8-1. Notice the box labeled A. Box A is operating in a product- or service-centric manner. The company culture is personality driven, based on the idiosyncratic behavior of the CEO, and the marketing and advertising efforts are driven primarily by creativity. This is why, in part, so many companies such as yours are in trouble. You can be sure that your successful competitors are embracing the digital age by leveraging tools that allow them to know more about their customers and yours, which gives them a tremendous competitive edge over competitors who base their strategy solely around their products or services. The simple fact is that the more you know about your customers, your competitors, and the overall market trends, the better decisions you can make on behalf of your company.

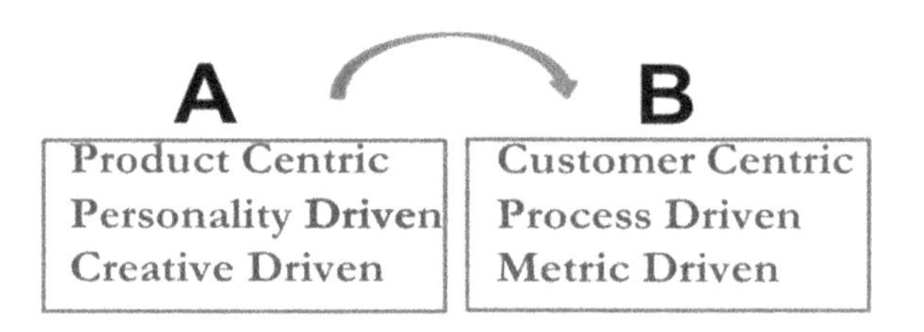

Figure 8-1. Predigital paradigm versus digital paradigm

Most founders and CEOs of companies in trouble today (in 2013) argue that they are in the mess in which they find themselves because of the Great Recession of 2008. The recession hurt hundreds of thousands of businesses as well as millions of workers, many of whom are still having difficulty finding jobs. However, one reason why the economy has recovered faster than many businesses is because these businesses have not made the necessary adjustments to the new realities of the marketplace. Many of these realities revolve around the fact that there is more competition in more sectors than ever before because companies have access to affordable tools, such as the Internet, social media, e-mail, and so forth. There has also been a general trend toward focusing on profitability (such as cutting expenses to increase margins by leveraging tools to work smarter with less staff) versus expanding market share at the price of profitability.

Simply stated, as illustrated in box B in Figure 8-1, in this digital age, it is critical that your business become more customer centric, process driven, and data driven. This does not mean that your company should no longer work on developing great products or services. It also does not mean that charismatic leadership that inspires and motivates employees is not important. Nor does it mean that creativity and innovation are not still needed to solve problems. However, it does mean that you need to pay more attention to which customers segments are most profitable for your company. It is also important to get feedback from your customers regarding not only what they think about your current product and service offerings, but also what products and services they would like to see your company offer.

Process driven, as reviewed in Chapter 6, means that there should be procedures established for every major process flow in your company, with standards and timelines adhered to with the aim of maximizing operational efficiency. When an executive or more senior person in a company, directly or indirectly, by a lack of action, tells a subordinate that he will get to a specific task when he is ready—versus when it is necessary for him to do so—his personality-driven style is detrimental to the company's success. In addition, when management is trying to solve a problem or trying to create a new product or service and it focuses solely on its creativity or gut feelings versus looking at hard data that show trends or customer survey feedback, it is not maximizing the company's chances for success.

As reviewed in Chapter 7, currently we have access to an incredible amount of information about our customers, which demands that we service them better, especially given the fact that product cycles are becoming shorter and shorter for many types of products. In addition, with an increasingly competitive marketplace, business operations must improve efficiency wherever and whenever possible. Finally, with rare exception, any marketing campaign that is not built on a set of metric assumptions and that is not managed and tweaked based on metrics is not going to be cost-effective. It is important to note that I am not saying the elements in box A in Figure 8-1 are no longer important. Of course they are. However, your business needs to be led by the elements in box B *complemented* by the elements in box A.

Don't Confuse Strategy and Tactics

It is a common mistake for management, which gets paid to drive tactics, to get strategy and tactics confused. After years of conducting strategic planning for companies, I always find myself needing to distinguish the two. Rather than provide an academic definition, I put the definition in the context of the company with which I am working.

At a high level, a strategy is an approach one takes to achieve the company's mission. It changes based on myriad circumstances, many of which have been reviewed in this book. Tactics are the elements used to implement your strategy. Often, companies that find themselves in serious trouble are relying on tactics that are not effective given the market dynamics. Furthermore, a strategy that does not take into account the constraints of the tactical elements available to a firm is not very pragmatic and does not have a very good chance of getting management and staff buy-in. The ideal situation is to have a balance between strategy and tactics based on your assessment of market forces and the financial and human resources available to your firm.

It is as much an art as it is a science to keep a balance between your strategy and your tactical plan. In your attempt to maintain this balance, it is critical that there be ongoing communication with management; otherwise, there will be confusion and frustration with policy changes. I experienced this situation firsthand when I was the executive vice president of strategic planning and marketing for CompuBank, NA, the first virtual bank in the country, back in the late 1990s. One of my responsibilities was to drive customer acquisition. In doing so, I convinced our CEO to allow me to hire someone dedicated to managing our affiliate marketing efforts. I was convinced that, because we were small and nimble, we could outflank our marketing counterparts at the big banks, who had to get their compliance department and/or legal departments to sign off on anything and everything they did. Having worked at a brick-and-mortar retail bank, I knew there was no way that compliance departments at big banks would let their heads of marketing work with third-party affiliates and have them have links with their logo on hundreds of web sites without conducting due diligence on each web site. The bet worked, and we became one of the fastest-growing banks in America, mostly because of the success of our affiliate marketing efforts. In addition, our cost per acquisition actually got cheaper before eventually leveling off, whereas the cost per acquisition for the big banks got more expensive over time, in part because they were relying on big ad campaigns.

Although the tactic of leveraging affiliate marketing worked, it ran its course. We proved to our investors that we could capture market share. However, we were in business to make money, so we also had to enroll profitable customers. After we captured a critical mass of customers and developed better metrics tied to these customers, it became clear that the some of our affiliate partners were good at bringing us customers, but these customers were not our ideal target segment.

Because our key investors demanded that our strategy evolve from solely grabbing market share to also focusing on profitability, our tactics needed to change as well. What was frustrating about this reality was that my colleague in charge of affiliate marketing did not understand the strategic shift initially and was frustrated that this very successful tactical initiative was being altered. Eventually, after reviewing the financials with him thoroughly, he bought in to the new strategy.

I mention this story because your strategy might need to change—even if the market is stable—because of other issues, such as investors' demands or competitive forces. This change may be frustrating for members of your team (even you!) who have put out a 110% effort to make an initiative successful. You and they may have a hard time accepting the fact initially that when your strategy shifts, so too must your tactical plan for your company to maximize its chances of success. Clearly, your overall strategy must shift if you are going to turn your business around.

Strategic Assessment

Whether you are selling to a business or to a consumer, the strategic assessment is the same even if your tactical approach differs. Having a great strategy but poor execution does not lead to success (Figure 8-2).

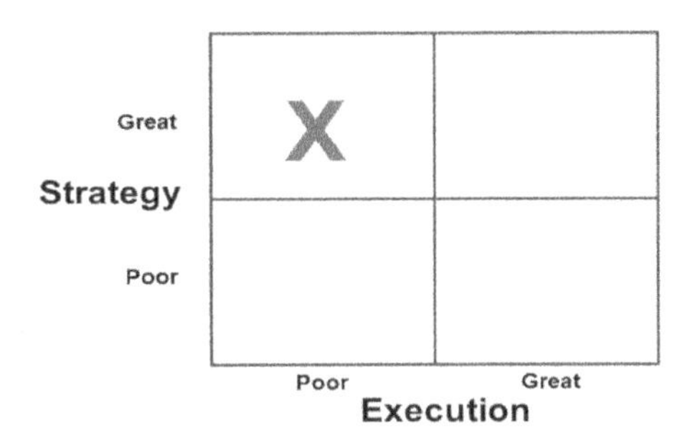

Figure 8-2. Great strategy with poor execution assessment

A lot of consultants, by the way, do a great job at helping their clients develop their strategic plans, but are not as successful when they go out on their own to run a business, in part because they have focused most of their careers developing and refining their analytical skills and have limited experience in executing sales and marketing plans or managing operations.

Let's now look at the opposite situation: companies that lack an effective overall marketing strategy but are good at ground-level tactics. Lots of businesses owners built their company based on their knowledge of a product and/or services as well as their ability to sell. They have great tactical skill. However, they simply don't have the strategic and financial skills and experience to overcome the business challenges they face when the market shifts beyond their experience zone. Smart and pragmatic CEOs recognize this and hire great talent to compensate for their weaknesses (Figure 8-3).

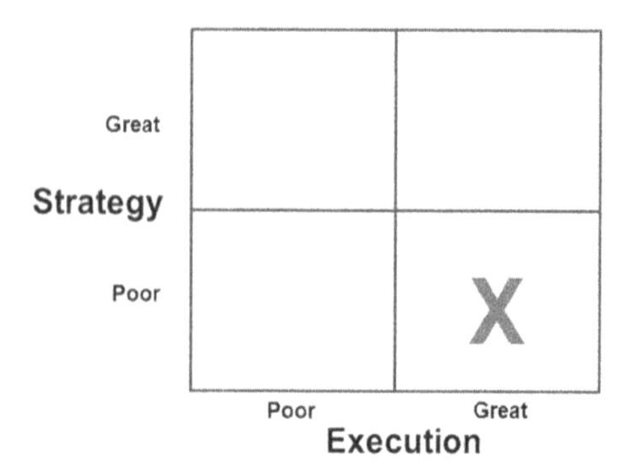

Figure 8-3. Great execution with poor strategy

Your firm may not be able to afford to hire great talent at this juncture. However, you can afford to listen to what your employees are learning and then to decipher what is relevant to your strategic planning needs. In addition, you may be able to afford to hire an outside consultant to help you get your company back on track. Experienced and effective consultants more than pay for themselves by either saving your firm money or by helping your firm make more money. Although not a guarantee for success, having a great strategy with great execution (Figure 8-4) certainly enhances a company's chances of success.

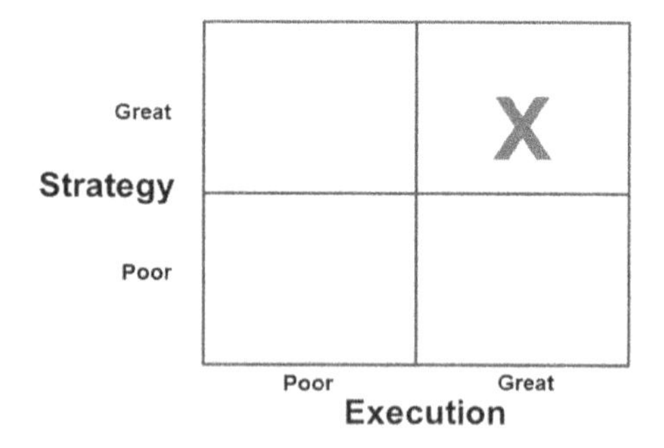

Figure 8-4. Great strategy with great execution

Tip Plan to review your strategy and tactics on a regular basis. The market is ever-changing, which means your strategy must as well.

Marketing Gap Assessment

I recommend that you conduct a marketing gap assessment, which exposes the inconsistencies in your strategy. It is important to understand that each of the boxes identified in the series of previous figures are equally important to your business, regardless of the fact that, at any given time, some take precedence over the others. As a result, the constraints of each category listed in Figure 8-5 have an impact on all the other boxes and vice versa.

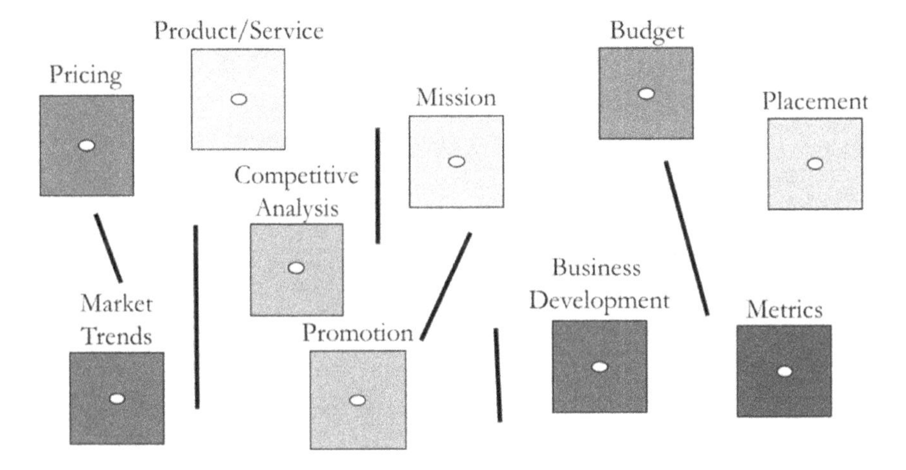

Figure 8-5. Poor coordination among key marketing elements

Figure 8-5 is a visual of the haphazardness of how most companies are coordinated. However, as shown in Figure 8-6, there should be one solid fluid line that connects the key elements. When these elements are not well coordinated (as in Figure 8-5), the consequences are an inefficiently run and most likely ineffective marketing effort.

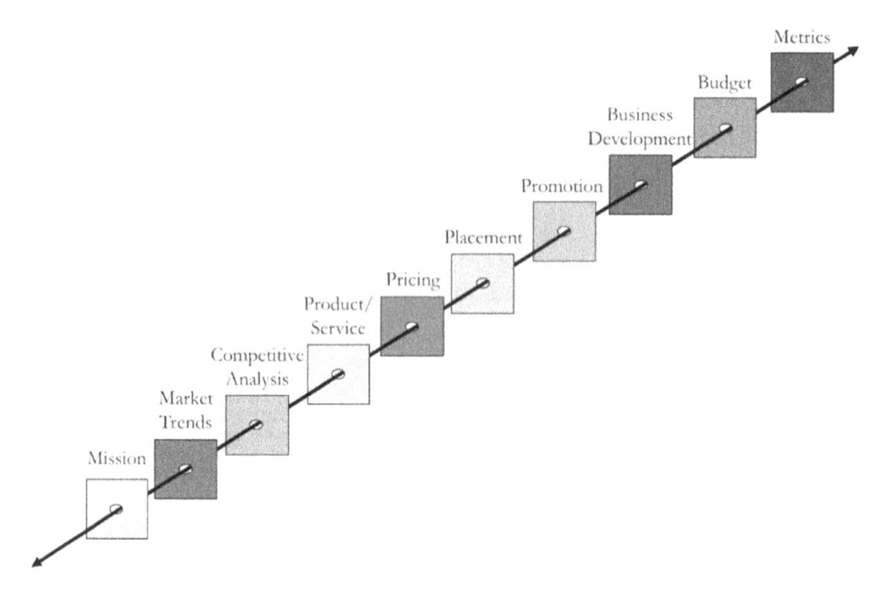

Figure 8-6. Visual of a well-coordinated marketing plan

Your task, along with the marketing manager, is to define goals, objectives, and critical success factors for each of the categories presented in Figures 8-5 and 8-6 in the context of their constraints, with the exception of Mission and Market Trends, which should have already been established by you. Thereafter, your marketing manager should make adjustments to each category based on the impact the constraints of the other categories have on each other. Closing the gaps with each of the other categories helps your company leverage the synergies more effectively between these critical success factors. This exercise, in turn, helps your firm maximize the returns on your marketing and sales efforts.

In Figure 8-6, I present the diagram in a more orderly fashion than its first iteration. Please note that the arrows go both ways to highlight the point that the interaction among these categories is a fluid process. Each category has its unique constraints as well as the ability to adjust based on the constraints of the other categories. You may want to add additional categories that are not included in my example.

It is important to note that you may want to add additional categories to this exercise that are not currently included in the example above. Another way of illustrating the point is to assume that each category above is a wheel on a bus. If some wheels are moving forward and some are moving in reverse, there is going to be friction. This is also going to be true if some of the wheels don't move at all and the other wheels have to pick up the slack. Let's review each of these categories.

Mission

Developing a mission statement, whether for internal use and/or to share with your customers, is important. If you already have a mission statement, review it to ensure that it still makes sense, given that the current situation of your company has changed since the original mission statement was written. The mission statement is not something you change very often; however, it needs to be realistic to have meaning to its intended audience.

The intent of a mission statement is to help define what your firm does and why. It needs to be short and to the point. Spending some time writing a mission statement or reviewing the one you already have will help you and your team to focus. Confirming what business you are in and what business you are not in is a great start to building consensus for your mission statement. If your team cannot agree what business you are in, how can it agree to the tactics needed to make your business successful? A mission statement might be as simple as stating what the company does, the value the company provides, or the purpose of the company's existence. An example of a mission statement is Nike's: To bring inspiration and innovation to every athlete in the world.

Market Trends

We reviewed the importance of marketing trends in Chapter 7. It is important that you review current trends periodically to be sure you have an understanding of the factors that drive your business. Is there still a market for your products and services? If not, you need to develop different products and services or you will soon be out of business. Do the market trends support the aspirations of your mission? If the market trends don't support your mission, go back and rethink your mission. It is critical that you have your hand on the current pulse of the market. Don't fall into the trap of thinking you know the market trends because you knew them several years ago.

Note Just because you were an expert on market trends a few years ago doesn't mean you are today. Stay on top of the market or it will smother you.

Competitive Analysis

We reviewed the importance of identifying your competitors in Chapter 7. Your competitors are subject to the same market forces as your business. Therefore, learning from them presents an opportunity to be more in touch with the market trends and to be more competitive. What do your competitors know that you don't? How do their actions in the marketplace reflect their understanding of the market trends? How do their products and services compare with yours? How does their pricing compare with your pricing? Where do your competitors sell their products? How do they promote their products? Knowing the answers to these questions helps you determine more effectively which products and services to sell, where to sell them, and how to price them.

Product and Services

Are you offering the products and services that your existing customers and your target customers want? How does the quality of your products and services stand up against your competitors' products? Based on the margins of your products and your inventory of each, which ones are you going to promote more aggressively? Is this consistent with current market trends? As discussed in the manufacturing section of Chapter 5, do you know the margins of your product? Do you have goals for each of your current products and services? Which products are causing you to lose money that should be eliminated immediately? Again, do not start spending money on marketing until you develop a thorough understanding of your position.

Pricing

Based on the quality of your products and services, your competitors' pricing, as well as overall macro economic trends, how does your pricing of products and services measure up? Is your pricing lined up with the expectations of your target customer base? Is your pricing consistent with the necessary margins required for the product to be profitable? Do not be afraid to slash prices to get rid of old inventory and to help generate much needed cash.

Also, don't be afraid to raise your pricing if your current pricing is below the market average and if your primary customer segment is not price sensitive. I experienced this latter point during a turnaround engagement with a high-end food business. Because of declining sales, the company's senior managers thought part of the company's problem was a result of its high prices. They thought their customers were price sensitive. They slashed their pricing because it was something that could be done practically with a stroke of a pen. However, this strategy cut into their margins and did not stop declining sales.

The reality was that pricing was not their problem. Their customer segment was not price sensitive, but quality and services sensitive, both of which had diminished. In addition, because of the expense of the high-quality ingredients used in the products, cutting pricing hurt margins dramatically. After improving the quality of their products and customer service, they actually raised the prices of these products with no adverse impact on sales. Make sure you really understand the genesis of your problems before you start to fix them.

Placement

Do you have consensus on who your target customers are? Do you have a primary, secondary, and tertiary customer base? Do you have clarity on who is *not* your desired customer and why? Based on these previous questions, are you sure that you are selling your products and services in the correct distribution channel and/or locations based on where your target customers shop?

Note Putting your products in front of the right customers is an art and a science. Start with the science (by predicting and then measuring results) and you'll develop your skills in the art of product placement quickly.

Promotion

Do you have a brand manifesto? If not, create one. First, define the emotional aspects of the experience you want your customers to experience with your brand. Does your logo (including, design, colors, and fonts) support your brand manifesto? Are you promoting your products and services to your target customers in a manner that is most effective given the distribution channel and location, and in the context of how your competitors' messaging toward the same target customer? Are you using images in your promotional campaigns that support your brand manifesto and are they appropriate based on your target customers?

One of the first things I do when I work with a new client is to collect every piece of collateral (business cards, brochures, folders, packaging, web site printouts, Facebook printouts, t-shirts, cups, stationary, and so on) that I can get my hands on. I then tape them to a wall. I always hope, for the client's sake, that all the collateral has the same look and feel. Unfortunately, they rarely do. I then bring the CEO into the room and ask him or her the following:

- Which logo is the official logo?
- Which colors are the official colors?
- Which tagline is the official tagline?

One would think this exercise would be quick. It inevitably ends up becoming a project to determine the answer to each one of these basic questions. Often, the head of marketing is brought into the room and cannot answer the questions either.

Knowing that the company's core branding is not consistent, I then do a similar exercise with the firm's advertising campaigns. I take as many ads I can get my hands on and tape them on the wall. I then ask the CEO to identify the company's target customers, such as male, female, rich, middle class, young, old, and so forth. I try to write on each ad who I think it is targeting. Again, there is inevitably a gap. This is an example of a company's imagery not matching its own sales data. When I point out these types of gaps to CEOs, I usually get a frustrated approval for my recommendation of halting all marketing activities until these gaps are bridged.

Tip Make sure the logos, messaging, and everything else you present to the outside world are simple and consistent.

Business Development

Although we examine business development in detail in the Chapter 9, start by asking yourself the following questions: Does your sales strategy complement your pricing, placement, and promotion strategy? Is your sales team well versed in the features and pricing of your products and services as well as those of your competitors? How well do they understand your target customers' needs as they relate to your products and services? Is your sales team aware of the promotional strategy? Does anyone on your promotional team talk to the sales team for insights on the feedback they are getting from customers?

Budget

Have you developed an appropriate budget to support your promotion and business development efforts? Conversely, have you adjusted your product development, promotion, and business development efforts based on your available budget? How often is your budget reviewed and adjusted based on the cash flow constraints the firm is facing? It does no good to develop an elaborate media campaign only to find out during the middle of the campaign that you don't have the budget to complete it. Good marketing campaigns are well thought out and well managed. Whenever I am engaged to help midsize and small businesses develop their marketing plan, I ask them to give me a budget that I can work with; otherwise, the plan becomes a meaningless exercise.

Metrics

There is a lot of truth to the phrase *If you can measure it, you can improve it.* Have you developed metrics to track each of your categories? If so, are you tracking the appropriate metrics, both qualitative and quantitative, to measure the progress of all the previous categories reviewed? How frequently are the respective metrics examined with your various internal stakeholders for the respective categories? Does your staff have an understanding of the respective metrics impact the company's financials?

When I ran the marketing effort for CompuBank, NA, we spent a tremendous amount of effort defining every metric we could think of that affected our ability to sign up new customers. Here are a few examples:

- How many ad impressions did we purchase for a particular campaign?
- What was the click-through rate?
- How long did a viewer stay at our site?
- On what pages did our viewers exit?
- What percentage of our viewers either logged in to an existing account or started to fill out an application?
- What percentage of those who started an application actually completed it?
- What part of the application did people stop filling out?

- What percentage of people who completed the application actually mailed in their deposit and signature cards?
- What percentage of mailed-in applications were incomplete? Of those incomplete, what was missing (such as the deposit and signature cards)?

Based on the answers to these questions, we created an ongoing action plan. We established a team that was responsible for improving the user experience on the web site. We also developed metrics that proved that it would be cost-effective for us to set up a second team that called applicants who had not completed their application to help them complete their application. As a result, we increased our closure rate dramatically in the incomplete application pool at a price per acquisition lower than the cohort that completed and mailed in all the necessary information on its own. The point here is that we developed a set of very granular metrics we could use to take action to improve the application process. Your marketing team should develop its own set of metrics that represents actions taken by your target customer necessary to achieve your end goal.

Putting the Pieces Together

It is not always easy to recommend how much money a firm should be spending on marketing, especially when it is having serious cash flow problems. You can look at industry comparables to determine what percentage of their budget other companies are spending on marketing. In addition, the stage of your company's development, and whether your client base is consumer or business, not only affects the size of your budget, but also affects the nature of your strategic plan. The size of your existing customer base affects your budget as well. Going after existing customers to spend more money on your products is usually always less expensive than acquiring new customers. The point in listing these various scenarios is to illustrate that every situation is different. You need to develop a budget based on your firm's goals and competitive landscape.

Regardless of how much it costs, your first step is to clean up your overall branding efforts. Great marketing looks simple to the intended audience; however, it takes a lot of planning and discipline to have tight, consistent, and effective product branding. By cleaning up your branding discrepancies, you help your staff members—whether they are in customer service, sales, or public relations—to be more effective in communicating a consistent message to your customers.

Also, focus on meeting existing client needs before going after new clients. You may already have a database with the names and contact information for your existing customer base. Your customers buy your products and/or services and, hopefully, have a positive experience doing so. If they have a negative experience and have shared it with your team, fix the issue. When you have eliminated the problem, contact your customers to tell them so, and entice them to try your product or service again by offering some type of incentive, such as a coupon.

If you currently use an outside marketing firm, even if you like it, hire an impartial consultant or a different marketing firm to help you conduct a marketing gap assessment. It is much easier for someone who has no history with your firm, and thus no vested interest with any of your branding efforts, to offer more constructive criticism about your marketing gaps. I have seen clients use a different firm for graphic design, advertising, newsletter development, and social media. In most cases, these firms are not in communication with each other. Each firm is trying to distinguish itself and is, indirectly, in competition with each other to get a bigger slice of the company's marketing budget. As a result, each is contributing inadvertently to the demise of the company, rather than to its success. I know this sounds harsh; however, the simple fact is that the primary goal of most of these firms is to generate their own sales. Whether they provide true value to their clients is a secondary issue. Therefore, it is the responsibility of your firm to manage your overall marketing strategy with each third-party company you engage to implement and/or manage a component of the tactical aspects of your marketing and to keep these vendors focused on your marketing objectives.

Summary

It is important to understand why developing an effective marketing strategy must be developed prior to developing an effective sales strategy. Marketing provides the "air cover" necessary to support a sales strategy. It is also important to understand the difference between strategy and tactics, which begins with evolving your marketing approach from being solely product centric, personality driven, and creative driven to one that is more customer centric, process driven, and metric driven. Your tactics might have to be modified to be more effective, given your revised strategy. Identifying and closing the gaps in the various elements of your marketing efforts should be conducted prior to spending money on any marketing campaigns. This gap assessment should include your mission, market trends, competitive analysis, profitability of your various products and services, pricing, placement, promotion, business development, budget, and metrics.

Engage a consultant or new marketing firm to conduct your marketing gap assessment to ensure the process is as unbiased and objective as possible. However, your firm is ultimately responsible for the development and management of your marketing strategy. When the gaps are closed, it is important that the critical elements of your marketing strategy be communicated to your sales team and customer service team. It is also important for your marketing team to garner feedback from your sales team and customer service team so that your marketing efforts can be adjusted appropriately to meet the needs of your customers more effectively.

Up next: Developing a more effective sales strategy.

CHAPTER

9

How to Develop a More Effective Sales Strategy

Never Underestimate the Difficulty of Developing and Managing a Successful Sales Strategy

This chapter's objective is to help you develop a more effective sales strategy. For most midsize and small companies, generating sales is the biggest challenge the company faces. You can succeed with your sales efforts if you have hard-working, competent professionals who are somewhat assertive, not afraid of rejection, and are driven financially.

When I conducted a search on Amazon for *sales strategy*, I received more than 20,000 results. Before you decide to read one of these books, conduct a gap assessment/audit of your current sales efforts. You can then use the results as a basis for a plan of attack to make ongoing, incremental improvements to your sales. There will be time later to revamp your sales strategy. For now, however, you need to develop a sales strategy in the context of the other challenges your company is facing, and you do this by focusing on asking the right questions.

Sales Is the Hardest Role in the Company

Many employees of companies with whom I have worked are jealous of their sales rep colleagues because the sales reps make more money than they do. Others see their sales colleagues coming and going; rushing to a breakfast, lunch, or networking event—all dressed up—and think their sales colleagues have an easy job. Nothing could be further from the truth, especially given your company's current predicament. Finding and keeping good sales reps is one of the hardest things to do in a company.

And what is so ironic is that the employees who are jealous of the sales reps never want to go into sales when offered the opportunity. In addition, a lot of CEOs don't want a sales job either. This is a big problem, especially because CEOs are generally the highest paid people in their company. It does not bode well for the future of any company if the head cheerleader does not have enough confidence and/or drive to lead the charge in selling. As the leader of your company, it is your role to lead the development of a sales strategy and to be involved actively in its implementation and subsequent performance tracking.

I often tell my clients' management teams that the sales reps in midsize and small businesses have the hardest job of any other role in the company. Then I get pushback from heads of various departments about how hard their team members work with very little recognition from other departments and management. This latter point is usually true and fixable, but the simple fact is that no other role in a company can be judged so objectively as a sales role. It's clear at a glance whether a salesperson is providing value to the company.

Simply stated, sales representatives are either closing business deals or they are not. They are either making calls and setting up meetings or they are not. All this activity is measured easily. Sales reps ultimately get paid for results, which can be quantified. This cannot be said for other roles in the company. At the end of the day, sales reps are at the mercy of a number of factors out of their control. They don't control the quality of the product, its pricing, its marketing, its competitor's offerings, the overall market trends, and whether a customer really wants or needs your products and services.

Identify Your Key Sales Problems

The first step in developing your sales strategy is to figure out and to develop a consensus regarding why your sales are not meeting your goals.

Why Are Sales Down?

There are a number of reasons your sales might be dropping. Chances are, it'll be the result of one or more of the following reasons:

- **Competitors:** Are your competitors outhustling your sales team? What are your sales reps hearing about competitors from customers? Are you aware of losing customers to your competitors? If you are competing against bigger and better funded competitors, have you determined your company's comparative strengths? Has your sales strategy incorporated these strengths into the company's messaging?
- **Economy:** The economy suffered in the Great Recession of 2008. However, many sectors have not only recovered, they are thriving (such as the fields of energy and health care). What are the trends in your sector? What are your sales reps hearing from their customers about the economy? If the economy is not a major factor in decreasing sales, it is important for your sales team to be aware that this is no longer a viable excuse for poor performance.
- **Full-time versus third-party agents:** Which of these two groups are producing more revenues? Are any of your third-party agents a negative influence on your full-time sales reps? It is possible that some of your third-party agents also represent your competitors and are garnering information from your firm to help them sell your competitor's products.
- **Marketing:** How current are your marketing pieces? What do your sales reps think about your marketing? Are they getting any feedback about your marketing from your customers? Are your marketers communicating with your sales reps?

- **Motivation:** How would you rank the morale of your sales team? Sales reps can be very temperamental. With your company facing so many challenges, what are you doing to increase team morale? Your best sales reps have probably already resigned. What are you doing to keep the remaining team members motivated?
- **Pricing:** How does your pricing stack up against your competitors? What type of feedback are your sales reps getting regarding pricing from your customers?
- **Product quality:** Is your sales team satisfied with the quality of the products it is trying to sell? What are your customers telling your sales reps about their satisfaction with your products? Are there major defects that have to be fixed before sales can increase?
- **Reps aren't being managed:** How much of your sales slump is a result of your team not being managed, supported, and held accountable for performance goals on a regular basis?
- **Reps aren't making calls to existing clients:** How much of your sales problem is as a result of your sales reps simply not staying in touch with existing customers on a regular basis?
- **Reps aren't prospecting for new clients:** How much of your sales problem is a result of your sales reps not putting enough effort into prospecting? Are they being provided with list of potential prospects in their territory?
- **Reps don't know products:** Do your salespersons really know the feature benefits of your products and services? Have they studied the collateral materials? Do they know how to sell each product and service correctly?

It is critical that you get feedback from every one of your sales reps regarding their opinion on why they think the company's sales are down and why, if indeed the case, their individual sales performance is down. I have interviewed a number of sales teams on various client projects and have always been amazed and delighted how candid the reps are with me. They are happy to explain why, in their view, the company's sales have decreased as well as why their own individual performance is not as effective as it could be.

Tip Sales down? Ask your sales reps why they think that is. They will probably be quite frank, so be prepared to hear things you may not want to hear. Then, act on them. Your company is at stake.

Conduct a Sales Audit

Just as you audited your marketing practices and results, so must you audit your sales efforts. The results of the audit will show you where you need to improve. The following subsections identify the components of a good audit.

Identify the Universe of Accounts

One of the first things to do when conducting the sales audit is to identify the universe of accounts (UOA) for each of your sales representatives. All sales reps should classify their accounts into a first-tier, second-tier, and third-tier rating based, in part, on past performance as well as on future expectations. Thereafter, they should be challenged to develop a simple strategy for selling to each of the three tiers of customers. There are probably fewer first-tier clients than second tier, and more second-tier than third-tier clients, which means it makes sense to spend more time with those able to generate the most business.

Here is an example of a strategy of a different kind for each of these categories of clients. Let's say you have a new push on product. Your reps will try to meet face-to-face with each of their first-tier clients, conduct a conference call or Skype call with each of their second-tier clients, and send an e-mail to each of their third-tier clients. Of course, a client in the second tier may evolve into a face-to-face meeting, just as an e-mail message to a third-tier client may evolve into a call and subsequent face-to-face meeting. By categorizing your customers, you are playing the odds as efficiently as possible.

Identify Universe of Prospects

The next step in the sales audit is to have each of your sales reps identify their universe of prospects (UOP). This process is similar to the UOA. All sales representatives should classify their prospective customers into a first-tier, second-tier, and third-tier rating based, in part, on the perceived similarities of these companies to the actual customers already tiered. Thereafter, they should be challenged to develop a simple strategy to sell to each of the three tiers of clients.

The sales strategy may be a bit different for prospective clients compared with current customers inasmuch as your reps won't have a prior relationship with the new prospects. Setting up a meeting may not be an easy task; however, it should be a goal for the tier one prospective clients. Another tactic is to send out a personal letter with sales collateral followed up with a phone call. The reps' strategy must be consistent, and then modified as they start to get positive and or negative results.

Tip Going after customers and prospects systematically yields results, but it takes discipline to get them. Having your sales force categorize its targets is the first step in creating a strategy to boost sales.

Review Performance

It is imperative that you give a performance review to the entire sales team so it has an understanding of where sales are today versus where they were in years past. It is also important that you set goals and expectations for the entire group and each individual.

It is also important that you conduct a sales audit on each member of your sales team regardless of whether they are a full-time employee or a third-party agent. The audit should include but not be limited to

- Their monthly performance for the current year and past annual performance for as far back as you can find the data
- The types of clients to which they have sold

- A demonstration of their knowledge of your products and services
- Their 30-second elevator pitch

Depending on the size of your sales team, I have no problem with you doing this audit with all the reps together. There is nothing like a little competition among sales reps to help increase collective motivation. I also find it effective to create a regular performance report that shows the year-to-date (YTD) performance of the company versus sales goals, as well as individual YTD figures versus individual goals.

Figure 9-1 is an example of this type of report for the first month of the year. It lists all the sales reps and their individual and collective results for the month of January. It also shows these same results on a quarterly basis as well as an annual basis, allowing the entire sales team to know exactly where each individual sales rep as well as the entire team stand regarding sales department and individual stated goals for any given month, quarter, and year.

Sales Reps	January	Monthly Goal	% of Goal Achieved	First Quarter Actual	Quarterly Goal	% of Quarterly Goal Achieved	Annual Actual	Annual Plan	% of Annual Plan Achieved
Alan Jones	110,000	100,000	110%	110,000	300,000	37%	110,000	1,200,000	9.2%
Bob Smith	80,000	83,333	96%	80,000	250,000	27%	80,000	1,000,000	8.0%
Cathy Brown	90,000	100,000	90%	90,000	300,000	30%	90,000	1,200,000	7.5%
Dorothy Oz	85,000	83,333	102%	85,000	250,000	28%	85,000	1,000,000	8.5%
Eric Evans	70,000	83,333	84%	70,000	250,000	23%	70,000	1,000,000	7.0%
Frank Stein	60,000	66,667	90%	60,000	200,000	20%	60,000	800,000	7.5%
Greg Gold	70,000	62,500	112%	70,000	187,500	23%	70,000	750,000	9.3%
Henry Hines	82,000	83,333	98%	82,000	250,000	27%	82,000	1,000,000	8.2%
Irwin Sanford	98,500	100,000	99%	98,500	300,000	33%	98,500	1,200,000	8.2%
Julie Brown	65,000	70,833	92%	65,000	212,500	22%	65,000	850,000	7.6%
Team Total	**810,500**	**833,333**	**97%**	**810,500**	**2,500,000**	**32%**	**810,500**	**10,000,000**	**8.1%**

Figure 9-1. Sample performance report for the sales team

KNOW WHEN YOU ARE BEING SOLD A BILL OF GOODS BY YOUR OWN REPS

Sales reps, by nature, are very independent people and do not like to be micromanaged. Some simply do not want to be accountable. If this is an issue you are experiencing with some members of your team, it is imperative that you rectify the situation immediately. The harder you come down on members of your sales team who have been neglecting their responsibilities (and thus have been taking advantage of your company), the sooner you will regain the respect and support you need from your remaining sales team to turn your sales around.

If you have third-party reps who are not making calls and setting up appointments, cut them loose immediately. They may be misrepresenting themselves on behalf of your firm to their personal advantage, not to the benefit of your company. You also do not have time to waste trying to convince reps already on your team why they should be putting out a 100% effort. Cut these individuals loose as well.

Evaluate Training

After you have an idea of your key problems and have conducted an audit on each of your sales rep's activities and the subsequent results, start the process of improving their individual and overall performance. First, you need to assess their knowledge in the following key success factors, then institute training in areas they are deficient.

Product Knowledge

How well does your sales team know the feature benefits of every one of your products and services and the associated pricing? It would be a mistake to assume that your sales reps have actually taken the initiative to learn the features and benefits of every one of the company's products and services they are responsible for selling. In addition, you do not want to take the risk of letting sales representatives figure this out for themselves. Their value is driving sales via the messaging developed by your marketing team—optimally with input from sales reps. Sales reps should not devise the marketing strategy. When sales reps invent their own messaging, there is inevitably one or two sales representatives who come up with inaccurate or inappropriate features and benefits for the product be sold.

After you've identified deficiencies in product knowledge, have someone on the product development team conduct training. Also, ensure (via the sales process flow) that sales reps are informed whenever there is a change to any feature of the company's products or services. The product alterations should be accompanied by a set of questions and answers that clients might ask of the reps.

Marketing Knowledge

How well does your sales team know the marketing campaign your customers and prospective customers are seeing? Do your sales reps know where they can find sales material to leave with their customers?

One of the most embarrassing situations for any sales representative is talking with a customer or prospective customer who knows more about a recent marketing campaign than the sales representative, who may have no idea what the customer is talking about. Not only should your marketing team work with your sales reps on informing them about upcoming marketing campaigns, but the marketing department should solicit feedback from various sales reps when they are in the process of developing a marketing campaign. This training should be conducted by someone on your marketing team, who should review the specific campaigns and the flight schedules for them.

Financial and Operational Constraints

How well does your sales team know the financial and operational parameters within which they must operate? Although it is absolutely essential that your sales reps be as aggressive as possible to generate sales, it is equally critical that they do it within the confines of your financial and operational constraints. It is imperative that your operational and finance team not only define these constraints, but also review them as part of sales training.

People in sales are, by definition, are pleasers. Because they live and die by customer satisfaction, they can be adept at stretching the truth a bit to snag the deal. Overpromising and underdelivering is a formula for a disastrous sales strategy. One example of such a promise is the delivery date of a product. Let's say a customer wants to purchase an item, but will do so only if the item can be delivered by or on a specific date. The sales representative, who wants to close the deal, promises the customer the company can deliver the product *without checking with the appropriate people* at headquarters to confirm whether the delivery date is realistic. When the production staff indicates it can't meet the deadline, the company is either going to have a disgruntled customer or the production team will have to work overtime to meet the deadline, thereby eating into the gross profit margins. Either scenario is bad and easily avoidable.

It is critical that the following sales policies, which are not all-inclusive, be determined and reviewed regularly as part of the process review:

- Range of product customization latitude
- Production timetable
- Delivery timetable
- Range for price negotiation
- Payment terms

Sales Knowledge

How well does your sales team actually know how to sell and close a deal? Do your reps know how to prepare for a meeting by doing due diligence on their client and/or prospect? Do they know appropriate dress and behavior etiquette? No doubt there are some deficiencies here. These issues should be addressed during the training conducted by your head of sales. If you do not have a head of sales, this training should be led by your most successful sales representative.

Regardless of whether you have a training budget, it is critical that your sales team have regular meetings that, in part, are focused on improving the team's ability to generate sales. These meetings may seem inconsequential but they are critical to the success of your business.

Analyze Your Sales Database

One of the tenets of your sales strategy must be to compile accurate metrics that are generated and reviewed on a regular basis. However, it is extremely difficult, if not impossible, to track metrics on a regular basis in a report format if you do not have a centralized database. If your firm does have a centralized sales database, you need to verify and then communicate to your sales team your expectations of what information they are expected to input and how often. The easiest way to hold your sales team accountable to inputting the necessary information is to inform the reps that they will not receive their commission checks until they have input the necessary information.

If you don't have a centralized database, the development of one should be the top priority in your sales strategy. You can sign up for `Salesforce.com` within a day, which is the easy part. The difficult part is to change your sales culture, which is most likely going to resist centralizing the sales process. Some of your sales reps will resist sharing their contacts in fear of losing them to another sales representative within the company. Others will resist migrating to a centralized system out of fear of being held accountable for their performance or lack thereof.

By having a centralized customer database that is eventually integrated with your accounting system, your company will be able to run various types of reports regarding customer performance trends as well as sales rep performance. You will also be able to create more granular types of reports based on any criteria that you capture in the database, whether it be gender, age, zip code, area code, industry, title, and so on. A centralized database also enables you to add new fields as you deem appropriate to enhance your reporting even further. The key is to continue to define the information you do not have that would help you manage your sales efforts better if you had it.

Note You are flying blind if you don't maintain a central sales database; it's the only way you can measure and track key performance factors. And you don't just need the right software and hardware—you need a sales force open to the idea of maintaining accurate data.

Regardless of the excuses posed by your team, it is imperative that you move forward on this strategy if you want to have any chance of improving your sales. In addition, by developing a centralized database, you are solidifying one of your most valuable company assets—customer information, which is the property of your company, not the property of your sales reps.

You will get valid pushback on this policy from third-party sales agents who have developed, at their own cost, client and prospect lists. They may be selling other products and services to their clients, and thus will not want to share their list. If your firm is paying for the list, you have a valid argument to require them to enter that information into your database.

Learn from Successes and Failures

Assess communication among salespeople as part of your sales audit. Regular communication is critical. In your turnaround phase, conduct a standing weekly sales call. If your sales reps are local, set up monthly face-to-face meetings. If your sales reps are national, set up a monthly Skype call.

It is important to identify the sales representatives that are having the most success and to determine whether the reasons for their success can be transferred to your other sales reps. Perhaps the sales reps that are having the best success are just lucky. They may have a territory that has a better microeconomy than the other sales territories. However, it could be that your most successful sales reps are doing some things that are responsible for their success. If this is the case, you certainly want those sales reps to explain their formula for success with other sales reps. It is important that all your sales reps share their success stories so that they can learn from each other.

You also want your sales reps to share horror stories so they can learn from each other. In addition, find out what your least-successful sales reps are doing that may be affecting their performance. You need to help them change their course of action.

Here's a story that illustrates the value of this type of sales audit. I was serving as an interim president of a company that needed outside management help in turning it around. We had a sales representative that would always come back from a meeting so excited that she just had a great meeting. I was spinning a lot of plates at the time and thus had not gotten to the point of a sales audit. At the end of one month, the representative came to me to complain about how little in sales commissions she was making. Initially, I was a bit confused and told her so, because she had often shared with me the positive responses she was receiving during her sales calls. When I asked her how many calls she was making to request a face-to-face appointment I was shocked to learn that she had an amazingly high success rate at getting a meeting and even getting business as a result of her meetings. Her problem, however, was that she was simply not making enough calls to request a meeting. At first she balked at the idea that she needed to be making at least 40 calls a day from an existing customer list to have the success she wanted. However, after we modified the compensation plan to include compensation for every live call completed, making the 40 calls a day became a no-brainer and her sales started to increase.

Set Clear Expectations and Sales Goals

Luck is when opportunity meets preparation. To get lucky in sales, you must establish a sales process and play the odds by monitoring it regularly with metrics. It is critical that part of your sales strategy entail stating sales goals and setting clear expectations from your sales reps. During your weekly status calls with your sales reps, set goals and objectives for the following week for each of your sales reps. Specifically, each rep should be aware of how many calls and appointments he or she is expected to make and attend. All reps should provide a weekly written update of the previous week's activities, including how many calls they made, how many meetings they attended, and how many sales they closed. The report should also include their game plan for next week to meet the stated goals. Reps should also note in the report any unforeseen challenges they faced the previous week that management and the rest of the sales team need to be aware of to be prepared to handle them in the most professional manner possible.

Tip Useful sales metrics to track include the number of prospecting calls made, the number of in-person visits, and the number of sales booked. Look, too, at the number of planned calls, visits, and sales versus actuals.

Make Sure Your Incentive Plan Is in Line with Your Goals

As your strategic plan evolves and you have a sense of your company's directional priorities, ensure your sales strategy and incentive plan is complementary. Analyze the two as part of your sales audit.

The two biggest complaints I hear from sales reps about what impedes their ability to generate sales is pricing and their commission rate. Given your company's need for cash, I suggest calling their bluff on both by dropping your prices and raising their commission rates for a set period of time to determine whether this gets you the desired results. This action sends a message to your sales reps that you want them to succeed. It also lets them know that you are taking their two biggest excuses off the table. If you don't get better results, you most likely have a sales rep problem rather than a pricing and commission problem.

Here are a few scenarios in which your incentive plan needs to be in line with your goals:

- If you have a large customer base, limited marketing dollars, and a short window in which to generate revenues, your priority should be to increase sales in your existing client base. Therefore, it is important to keep your sales reps focused on your current client base, not on new clients, which may involve a longer sales cycle. Whatever sales incentive or contest you create to increase sales needs to be in line with this goal, with a disincentive for going after new clients.
- If you are in the retail or food and beverage business, you may have a large, active customer base that isn't difficult to grow, but you may find your average sale per ticket is not high enough. Hence, your incentive plan should focus on enticing your in-store personnel to be more proactive in upselling to your customers. This not only entails some type of incentive but also some sales training on how to upsell certain products when a customer is buying a standard product.
- If you are in a business such as Internet services or residential energy, where losing customers on a monthly basis is part of the reality of your business model, your incentive plan needs to encourage the acquisition of new clients.
- You may want to get rid of old excess inventory of a product you are no longer going to carry. Hence, you may want to consider a special bonus/incentive to encourage your sales reps to find a buyer.

The bottom line is that your sales reps are motivated by money. This is a good thing, because they are the primary way in which your firm generates sales. Therefore, it is important that you leverage this fact by developing, managing, and tweaking an incentive program that drives the types of sales within the desired time frame you seek. If you are not getting the results you want you from your sales reps, review the current incentive plan.

Summary

Never underestimate the difficulty of developing and managing a successful sales strategy. Sales is the hardest role in most companies; its performance can be assessed more objectively than any other role in a company because the metrics of success are very simple—you either generated sales or you did not.

The first step in developing a sales strategy is to conduct an audit of why the current sales are not meeting expectations. A number of factors—including the economy, full-time versus third-party agents, marketing, motivation, pricing, product quality, management, and daily tasks—should be evaluated to determine where more effort needs to be allocated. All of your sales reps should identify their UOA and segment it into three tiers. Thereafter, they should do the same for their UOP. These tasks should be followed by a performance audit of each sales rep. After the audit is conducted, hold your sales reps accountable for their performance or lack thereof.

To start the process of improving sales, conduct a training audit, including but not limited to product knowledge, marketing knowledge, financial and operational constraints, and sales knowledge. It is critical that your sales strategy include a centralized database that enables you to track your sales reps' activities and results via regular reporting. It is also important that your sales team learn from its respective successes and failures to make the team more effective. There should be no doubt regarding your expectations and goals for each sales rep; they should be documented and tracked by the centralized database. Last, it is important that your incentive plan line up with your strategic goals to focus your sales reps.

Up next: How to manage your board of directors and investors better.

PART

IV

Managing from the Top Down

CHAPTER

10

How to Manage Investors and the Board of Directors Better

Total Transparency Is Critical

This chapter's objective is to help you manage your investors and board of directors better. Chances are that you have not been managing either as effectively as you could. Although this is completely understandable given all the other problems with which you have been dealing, this oversight is not prudent or helpful in your efforts to turn your company around. No one likes to be the bearer of bad news, especially if you are the captain of the ship, and any self-respecting entrepreneur is going to find it difficult to look at his or her investors in the eye and tell them that, although you gave your best effort, the results have been less than satisfying. I have been there and know how it feels. I once raised seed capital for a startup that did not work. Although I am disappointed with the results of my investors' money—even after more than a decade—I feel satisfied that I was transparent about all the company matters throughout the entire life of the deal.

The point is, regardless of how infrequently you have communicated with your investors and board of directors in the past, you must start immediately to have regular discussions and provide news and numbers with complete transparency. Regular communication with your board and investors is not only part of your fiduciary responsibility as head of your company, but it also may help you garner the necessary resources (financial and human) necessary to turn your company around.

Tip Your board and investors are extremely interested in the state of your company. Keep the information flowing. There's no such thing as overcommunicating in a turnaround situation.

Put All the Bad News on the Table ASAP—All of It

Your first step in being more transparent is to request a meeting with your board of directors, followed by a meeting with your investors. If you do not have a board of directors, hold the meeting with your investors. In preparation for one or both of these meetings, develop a two-page memo that outlines the key successes and challenges the company has been facing since your last communiqué to them. This memo should include, among other things:

- A summary of the company's financial performance
- Your approach to turning the company around
- Where you need their assistance
- The date, time (not to exceed 90 minutes), and location of your meeting as well as a dial-in number for those who cannot attend in person
- An exhibit containing
    - Current profit-and-loss sheet
    - Current balance sheet
    - Current aged accounts payable report
    - Current aged accounts receivable report

If you have a board of directors, the memo to your investors may need to be modified based on input from your board of directors meeting. The memo to your investors should also be signed by the board of directors. This action communicates to your investors that your board is aware of the company's predicament and supports your proposed plan of action.

Your first couple of memo drafts should be focused less on length and more on containing all the information you want to communicate. Thereafter, it may take you several drafts to consolidate your core material to a few pages. The brevity will give your investors a clear picture of the company's predicament and your plan moving forward. Just to clarify, your memo should state the process you will take to develop a plan to turn the company around. The process should be based in part on the recommendations made in this book as well as ideas you've gleaned from other sources. Inform the board that you'll send a follow-up memo that outlines the key components of your strategic plan after it is completed. In addition, have your attorney and/or close advisor review the memo before you send it.

It goes without saying that this memo is a very important document that requires your best effort. The memo should be as professional as possible. Put as much time in to writing it as necessary. Do not sugarcoat the company's problems, and do not be defensive. Touch on all the major problems the company is facing without going into the details of each one. You will have an opportunity during the meetings to address questions about specific problems.

Don't be afraid to admit mistakes. Chances are, the poor economy has had a significant negative impact on your business, and it probably has exposed other systemic problems. The key is to show your investors you have learned from previous mistakes—in part by the approach you will take to get the firm back on its feet.

Be candid with your investors. Let them know there is a high probability that implementing your strategic plan requires additional capital. Note that—depending on the terms of your private placement memorandum—your existing investors will have first right of refusal to invest more money in your company, based on a prorated basis. Those who choose not to invest additional capital will have their existing ownership percentage of the company diluted. Those choosing to invest then have the ability, on a prorated basis, to buy additional shares that were allocated originally to the investors who chose not to reinvest.

There may be areas other than providing additional capital where your investors may be able to help. Some of your investors may be able to make some key introductions on your behalf to key sales prospects; others may be on good terms with some of the vendors to which you owe money and thus can help renegotiate terms. You might have a few investors who want to help you review and tweak your strategic plan. Propose these other-than-financial investments in your memo.

Tip Put your investors and board members to work. Ask them to help you get sales, make introductions, provide expert advice, or whatever else you need. It's in their best interest to comply with your requests.

Example of Board of Directors Memo

Figure 10-1 is an example of a memo sent to a board of directors. Note the approach, but tailor it your unique situation.

Confidential Memorandum

January 5, 2013

To: Newco Board of Directors
From: Jonathan H. Lack, CEO, Newco
Re: Board of Directors meeting, 1/27/2013, Noon–1:30 PM, Newco Headquarters

In preparation for a Newco investors meeting I would like to hold on from 5:00 PM to 6:30 PM February 17, 2013, at Newco's office, I would like to convene a board of directors meeting on January 27, 2013, at Newco's office from noon to 1:30 PM. The purpose of the board of directors meeting is to review the agenda items to be discussed at the investors meeting and to garner input from the board of directors regarding the best way the company can achieve its mission and vision. Please see the attached a letter to the investors that I would like to review during the board of directors meeting. Please confirm via e-mail (jlack@roi.com) and/or phone (713-123-4567) if you are able to attend the board of directors meeting and/or if you are able to dial in to the meeting via conference number 1-800-132-4567, code 1234. I look forward to a constructive meeting.

Thanks!

Figure 10-1. Sample board of directors memo

Example of Investors Memo

Now that you've written the memo to your board, get to work on a memo for your investors that outlines the problems the company is facing. An example of an investor memo is presented in Figure 10-2.

Confidential Memorandum

January 5, 2013

To: Newco Investors
From: Jonathan H. Lack
Re: Newco Investor meeting, 2/17/2013, 5:00 PM to 6:30 PM ,Newco headquarters

Newco's next investors meeting will be held February 27, 2013, from 5:00 PM to 6:30 PM at Newco's office. The point of the meeting is to provide investors with an update of Newco's progress this past year and to garner your support for future initiatives. In preparation for the February 27th meeting, I would like to give you an update on Newco's successes and challenges since my last investors memo.

Despite the challenges that Newco has faced this past year, which I review later, I remain optimistic about Newco's ability to compete in the marketplace. Our segment's recovery remains sound. Industry experts have noted 5% average annual growth during the past several years, and our segment is predicted to grow at 6% during the next several years.

During this past year, Newco had several successes that give me confidence about our longterm potential. Here is a list of our major achievements:

1. We won a large order from Whizco, market leader in the automotive after-market.
2. We got good press for our new cloud product, including a mention in the *Wall Street Journal.*
3. Besides the new cloud product, we introduced two other new products and upgraded three others.
4. Jim Schmidt, our new business development director, has really hit the ground running, bringing in not only the new Whizco account, but four others that have placed five-figure orders and two that placed six-figure orders.
5. Our overhead decreased by 12% thanks to closing some facilities and trimming the workforce in a few spots. We also discontinued two products, which reduced our losses as well.

Despite our successes, Newco is, however, still recovering from a number of setbacks that arose during the past several years:

1. As the attached financial statements show, our sales have not recovered since the 2008 recession. Last year, our sales were $10,000,000, a slight 2% increase from 2011 but still a full 10% off our peak of $11,111,111 in fiscal year (FY) 2008.
2. As a result of our flat sales, we have accrued $3,000,000 of debt, which has limited our free cash flow to develop other areas of the business.
3. Last year, we launched our new security product, in which we had made a significant investment of time and money. Unfortunately, market acceptance was not on par with our expectations, most likely the result of a limited marketing budget.
4. We also lost our vice president of sales to a competitor, which hampered our ability to enter new markets.

(continued)

As a result of these challenges, Newco faced a loss of $1,500,000 for FY2012 (see exhibits A and B, a current balance sheet and profit-and-loss statement, respectively). Subsequently, management has decided to undertake a strategic planning process led by an experienced outside consultant, John Doe. This planning process entails reviewing every aspect of our business to help us determine not only where we can reduce our operating expenditures, but also how we should reposition Newco in the marketplace and move forward, given the ever-changing market dynamics.

This planning process will take between 60 and 90 days to complete, and includes the following:

- Ways in which we can manage our cash flow better, including our account payables and account receivables
- Ways in which we can manage our employee productivity better
- Ways in which we can manage our technology, facilities, and manufacturing better
- Ways in which we can integrate our various workflows in a more synergistic manner
- Ways in which we can develop a more comprehensive marketing and sales strategy
- Ways in which management can work smarter

I am committed to making a concerted effort not only to keep you, our investors, better informed of the company's progress, but also to leverage the various resources that, collectively, you may have to offer. Specifically, in the short-term, I need assistance in negotiating with our vendors to whom we owe money and with our customers who owe us money. Please let me know if you have a goodrapport with anyone on either list. In addition, I need assistance with one of our landlords, ABC Realty, who is resisting our attempts to terminate a lease on a location we do not need. I also need assistance with First Bank in an attempt to renegotiate our loan. I'd love to have some help overcoming these challenges.

I am looking forward to discussing these issues with you either before or during our upcoming meeting. Please confirm via e-mail (jlack@roi.com) and/or phone (713-123-4567) if you are able to attend the investors meeting. If you can't attend in person, you can dial in to the meeting via conference number 1-800-132-4567, code 1234. I look forward to a constructive meeting.

Thanks!

Figure 10-2. Sample investors memo

Prepare for the Meeting

Although you should be prepared for both the board meeting and the investors meeting, let's focus on preparing for your investor meeting. The first step is to reach out directly to every one of your investors to ask the following questions:

1. Did they receive your memo?
2. Do they have any questions?
3. Will they be attending the meeting and/or dialing in?
4. Has any of their contact information changed?

To ensure your meetings go as smoothly as possible, it is important you remove any elements of surprise. Ironically, this could come from you if an attendee has not read the memo before the meeting and is hearing bad news about the company for the first time. Therefore, verify that every investor has received and read your memo. You also don't want someone asking basic questions during the meeting that are answered in your memo, which will hamper the pace of the meeting and could put you off your agenda. In addition, you don't want to be blindsided by an irate investor who has read the memo but wants to share his or her disappointment in your performance in front of all the other investors.

As mentioned, talk to your investors before the meeting. During your conversations, thank them for their investment and for their patience. Be as courteous as possible; arguing does not reflect well on you. Be as good a listener as possible. Reassure them that their points are well taken and that you are doing everything possible to protect their investment. If you do not know the answer to a question asked by an investor, let him or her know you will determine the answer and convey it before the meeting. Such questions are often related to the financial aspects of your business, and you may require your chief financial officer's input.

Note Always confirm with investors that they received your memo and ask whether they have any questions. Head trouble off at the pass, if you can, before the meeting.

Take notes during each conversation so you address the issues your investors raise when you follow up with them. Keep a record of who you spoke with and when, as well as any specific matters you reviewed that need further clarification and/or follow-up. Figure 10-3 provides an example of call notes.

Investor Call Notes January 2013					
Last	First	Date Called	Attending Investor Meeting	Dialing In	Notes
Jones	John	15-Jan-13	Yes	-	Wants to see last year's financials
Smith	Sam	15-Jan-13	No	Yes	Wants to know how much money we need to raise
McDonald	Kathy	16-Jan-13	No	No	Wants to know when K-1s will be mailed out

Figure 10-3. Sample investor call notes

Develop a Meeting Agenda

Develop an agenda for your meeting that follows the outline of your memo. Have copies of the agenda and your memo for your attendees as well as any additional handouts you deem appropriate. Make sure to remember to e-mail any handouts to those who are dialing in to the call and to those investors who could not take part. It is important that you review everything you are going to discuss during the meeting in advance of the meeting so you are familiar with the various issues to be discussed and are comfortable talking about them. In this way, you present yourself as being in charge of your company. In addition, before the meeting, decide how much time to allocate to each agenda item to ensure the meeting finishes on time. Review your notes from the premeeting investor calls. Anticipate any questions you might be asked by the attendees.

Get a good night's sleep before the meeting so you are at your best. Assign a staff member to make sure your summary presentation of the issues outlined in your agenda is loaded in advance and check the overhead projector equipment to make sure it's working properly. The last thing you want is to have technical difficulties with a projector and/or Internet connection, which could have been fixed before the meeting. I have seen this happen several times. Not only is it quite embarrassing, but it sets a bad tone for the meeting. It is also important that you assign one of your staff members to take thorough notes during the meeting. Serve refreshments, but no alcohol.

During the meeting, do not make promises you cannot keep. At this phase of the game, your investors are wary (and weary) of promises. Note also that, although your investors have a right to be frustrated and even mad, they do not have a right to be verbally abusive or obstructive to your running the meeting. Therefore, depending on the nature of your business and/or size of your board and investors, you may want your attorney present to help run any interference with an irate investor or board member, which can alleviate a lot of the pressure you are going to feel. If you don't have an attorney present, let your investor know that you are happy to set up a meeting to further discuss the matter with them but that you would like to continue with stated agenda.

Managing the Meeting

Start the meeting as close to the stated starting time as possible after you have a quorum for your board meeting or 75% of those who confirmed their attendance for your investors meeting. Even if you don't have 75% of those confirmed present, begin no later than 10 minutes after the stated start time. No one will be offended that you start the meeting on time.

However, if the meeting runs over the allotted time, some of your attendees who have other commitments may be annoyed. Although many in attendance may be friends, this is a business meeting, not a social gathering. Hence, the meeting should be managed accordingly.

Begin by thanking everyone for attending and then stating the meeting objectives. Your stated objectives can be as simple as

- Reviewing, at a high level, the memo you sent
- Answering questions about any aspect of the memo
- Making requests/pleas for help from board members or investors
- Discussing your requests
- Summarizing your next steps, including how and when you are going to follow up with everyone who attended as well as those who could not attend

Have unstated personal objectives for the meeting as well:

- Impress on your investors that you are still willing and able to keep fighting for their investment.
- Impress on your investors that you have learned from mistakes, that there is a positive future for the company, and that it is worth the board members investing more of their time and the investors investing more of their money.
- Impress on your investors that you are developing a strategic plan.

It is important to stick to the appropriate amount of time you budgeted for each agenda item during your meeting preparations. Make sure that you leave enough time for questions to be asked and answered at the end of the meeting. When you get close to the designated finish time, let everyone know that you will take one more question before the meeting is adjourned and that you will be happy to stick around as long as any of your investors would like to ask any other questions.

If you know when your strategic plan will be completed, suggest a couple of dates and times for your next investors meeting, which should be held as close to the completion date of the plan as possible. Make sure you take holidays into consideration when scheduling the next meeting. Most investors in attendance will have a smartphone that will allow them to check their availability on the proposed date. Be as amenable as possible to everyone's constraints, but have a goal of locking in a date and a time before the meeting is adjourned. It is very rare that everyone will be able to attend the selected date, which is why it is important that you call everyone before and after the meeting, especially those who cannot attend or dial in.

Before adjourning the meeting officially, recap the major themes/agenda items discussed and any outstanding matters to be determined via a future conference call or through e-mail. Thank everyone for coming and let them know you will be following up with them in the coming days. After the meeting adjourns, do not get into a lengthy conversation with any of your investors. Thank them for coming before they walk out the door. The investors you were not able to greet before the meeting should be your primary targets to thank. It is important that you connect personally with as many of your investors in the room as possible. You're there to inform and also to sell the future of the company.

Tip Don't get bogged down with any one investor after the meeting. Thank each one for coming to the meeting and for making an effort to help turn things around.

Meeting Follow-up

The day after the meeting, send out a memo that summarizes the meeting for all investors. The memo summary should include

1. Matters discussed from the agenda
2. Pertinent questions asked by board members or by investors, depending on the meeting
3. Follow-up action items agreed to during the meeting
4. Date and time of the next investors meeting

Thereafter, it is important that you follow up with each investor to garner feedback from the meeting and the summary memo. At this point, you are in sales mode; you probably have to ask your investors for more capital. If and when you undertake your next round of fund-raising, communicate to your investors how they get a return with their new investment and what happens to their existing investment if they do or do not participate in the next round of financing.

Leverage Your Investors

Your investors invested their hard-earned money into your company either because they believed in the original business plan and/or they believed in you. Regardless of their reasons for initially investing, all of them want to get a return on their investment and see you and your team succeed during the process. Depending on the nature of your business, some of your investors may be able to help open up some doors for business development, others may be able to help you negotiate with some of the vendors to which your company owes money, and still others might be able to find some additional investors.

Most likely, the worst is behind you and the company. A new strategic plan is going to provide the company with some immediate wins. Success breeds success. Send out a monthly update to your investors as a way of keeping them engaged and excited about your progress. These communications will allow future investors meetings to run smoothly, because everyone will be up to date on the company's progress.

Summary

Remember that total transparency and regular communication, whether it be monthly or quarterly, is the best way to keep your investors informed and engaged. Your board of directors and investors are assets that you should try to leverage as much as possible. Respect your directors' and investors' time and money. Never underestimate the importance of being prepared for each investor call or meeting. Put the necessary effort into documenting the successes and challenges the company is facing in a constructive and professional manner. Your investors want to get a return on their investment, and they want you and your team to succeed.

Up next: How to manage your turnaround consultant.

CHAPTER

11

How to Hire and Manage Your Turnaround Consultant

Don't Be Afraid to Seek Help and to Act on the Advice

You may decide, after reading this book, that you simply do not have the bandwidth or expertise to lead the strategic planning/turnaround process. This chapter's objective is to help you manage the process of hiring and managing a turnaround consultant. I must admit upfront that I am somewhat biased about this process, having been an entrepreneur who could have used a turnaround consultant at one point in my life, and I have been engaged by a number of clients to do the various tasks discussed throughout this book.

Setting Your Own Expectations

Before you start looking for an outside consultant to help you turn your company around, it is important that you have clarity regarding what you hope the consultant can do for you. Here are some questions to consider:

1. Do you want the consultant to make her own assessment of what your company's problems are and provide solutions?
2. Do you want the consultant to provide solutions to specific problems you have already identified?
3. Do you want the consultant to help implement her recommended solutions?
4. Do you want the consultant to serve in an "interim president" role—and have some real authority—to guide your team through the turnaround process?
5. Do you want the consultant to provide you with a strategic document?

Perhaps hiring an outside consultant was not your idea, but something that was strongly encouraged or even imposed by your investors or board of directors. If this is the case, I can guarantee you that you will be wasting the company's money and precious time if you don't support this opportunity 100%. This does not mean that you have to agree with all the consultant's recommendations. It does mean, however, that if you are at all resistant to an outside, seasoned professional coming in with the sole objective of finding ways in which to help you turn around your company, you will inevitably—consciously or subconsciously—undermine her efforts. Sure, you will win the battle, and the consultant will either quit or not be reengaged after the initial work. However, you will lose the war of turning your company around, because you will be letting your ego and pride get in the way of making sound business judgments.

I have been in this situation more than once. Frankly, I found the CEOs' behavior selfish and irresponsible given, the fact that employees' livelihoods were at stake, not to mention shareholder investments. Shareholders often are family members, friends, or qualified investors, so you must take them into consideration as well. As CEO, you have a fiduciary responsibility to maximize the value of their investment.

Given the situation of your firm, you have very little to lose by working closely with an outside consultant. You may even be pleasantly surprised and somewhat relieved to have an outside professional come in to your company and help you turn it around. Who better to appreciate the challenges you are facing than someone who is experienced in dealing with such issues.

Tip Consider hiring a consultant who specializes in turnaround situations. This person will understand your predicament better than anyone.

Important Selection Criteria for a Turnaround Consultant

If you choose to hire a consultant, you'll need to consider a variety of factors. Here's a rundown.

Experience

Consultants usually sign nondisclosure agreements so they are not able to tell you the details of what they did for specific clients. They should, however, be able to describe in writing and/or verbally the different types of situations in which they have been brought in to help, without divulging any confidential information. Turnaround consultants can also provide you with references from previous clients, who may provide you with details regarding the situation for which they were hired.

It is not always critical that consultants come from within your industry. They do, however, need to have extensive experience in working with distressed businesses. Make sure they have the appropriate training (e.g., MBA, CPA, CFA, etc.) and at least 10 years of practical experience on which to draw. There are pros and cons of hiring a consultant with extensive experience in your industry. Clearly, the pros are that she is going to have a clear understanding of your sector's ebbs and flows as well as have key contacts that may come in handy. The downside of hiring someone with years of experience in your industry is that she is somewhat biased and does not have experience from other industries on which she can draw.

Tip Evaluate your current situation and look for the strengths in a prospective consultant that best matches your immediate needs. Then, hire that person.

Proposal

How you answered the five questions posed at the beginning of this chapter may help you determine whether you want to develop a request for proposal (RFP). This document outlines formally what you are seeking from a consultant. The advantage of an RFP is that you can post it on a job board such as Indeed, Simply Hired, or LinkedIn in the hopes of getting a large response without having to talk initially to every prospective consultant. The downside of this approach is that you may not want the general public to know about your problems, and you may get a lot of responses from candidates that did not read the RFP correctly and are not qualified for the tasks you need done.

You may prefer to bypass the RFP process and see what your prospective consultants propose based on their discussions with you. One advantage of this approach is that it allows consultants to ask you more questions up front. Then, their proposal is more likely to be tailor-made to your situation.

A good proposal should have the following elements:

1. **Background understanding:** This section of the proposal should state the consultant's understanding of what your firm does and your firm's current predicament. This helps put into context why the consultant is proposing her particular methodology.
2. **Objectives:** This section should list the objectives the consultant believes that, once achieved, will solve your problems.
3. **Phase I:** This section should detail the specific activities the consultant proposes to do to achieve the stated objectives, such as conduct interviews, conduct market research, conduct financial analysis, and so forth. It should include the methodology involved to achieve the tasks and with whom in your firm the consultant may need to communicate.
4. **Phase II:** This section should detail specific work to be done, in part based on findings from phase I, along with feedback from phase I by management. Phase II can also be determined based on the recommendations the consultant makes during phase I.

5. **Summary of deliverables and fees:** This section should have an itemized summary of what is going to be delivered and when, along with the proposed fees.
6. **Terms and conditions:** This section should state the consultant's terms and conditions for taking on this project. It typically explains what portion of the payment is due when, as well as the policy for out-of-pocket reimbursement expenses such as preapproved travel expenses, market research, Kinko's/FedEx, and so forth.
7. **References:** This section should contain references with contact information listed.
8. **Biography:** This section should have the bio of the consultant attached to it. You may have already met with each of your consultant candidates, during which time they talked about their background and experiences. However, you may need to forward the proposals to your board of directors, who have had no contact with these candidates and will want to read about their background.

A really good proposal is straightforward and details specific action items the consultant proposes to undertake. There should be no ambiguity regarding what is being proposed, how long it will take to complete, what the final deliverables will be, and the cost of the project. An experienced consultant knows that you may want to tweak parts of the proposal either by deleting something and/or adding something. After these edits are incorporated and you are ready to sign, there should be no misunderstanding about what is going to happen and when.

Selection Process

A big part of your selection process should be based not only on the proposal but also on an interview with the prospective consultants. A face-to-face interview is always ideal. However, there is a good chance that some of your top candidates may not be based in your city. You can either fly the candidate in for a day at your expense plus their consulting time for a day or you can have a phone or Skype interview. Regardless of which medium you choose to conduct your interview, it is critical that you come away with a feeling of rapport and a sense of trust. This person is going to find out a lot about you over a several-month period. She has to garner your trust in a very short period of time to walk you through a process that is going to be extremely uncomfortable for you, even if it is in your best interest. The challenge you have is choosing someone who tells you what you *need* to hear, not what you *want* to hear. However, she needs to do this in a nonthreatening manner.

Have your top management and board of directors meet and interview your top candidates. The more buy-in you have with the candidate you end up selecting, the better chance you have of making the engagement work.

Tip To get buy-in from your board members, managers, and investors, introduce the candidate to them and let them ask questions. You—and your consultant—need all the support you can get.

Introducing the Consultant

After you have selected a consultant and signed a contract, have a meeting with your top managers and key staff to introduce the consultant. It is absolutely critical that you, as the CEO, let your management team know that you are behind this initiative 100%. Regardless of what you think, your management team is going to be somewhat skeptical that you are really going to listen to the recommendations of an outside consultant. You need to impress on them why, this time, things are different and/or why you believe the timing is right for someone on the outside to come in and help management turn the business around.

It is equally important that you impress on your management team that they need to be behind this initiative 100% as well. They need to cooperate with your consultant and provide her with any information requested. In addition, managers must let their direct reports know they back this initiative and they expect their team members to be supportive of the consultant's requests for information and for their time for confidential interviews.

It is also important to communicate to both management and staff that the consultant has signed a confidentiality agreement and is merely collecting information. The consultant will not give direction to staff members regarding any operational issues. If the role of the consultant changes later, the CEO should make a formal announcement of this role change to alleviate any potential confusion and misunderstandings.

It may be natural for some of your top managers to be a bit skeptical regarding the value an outside consultant can provide. Any experienced consultant knows how to handle these types of personalities, who in many instances end up becoming her biggest supporter. However, I experienced a situation in which a manager was resistant to many of my recommended changes that were no-brainers. He was given ample opportunity by the owner to get on board with the program; however, he would not comply and was terminated.

Regular Updates

Although it is important that you allow your consultant the room to dive in to the project as outlined in her proposal, it is also important that you stay in regular contact with her. A good consultant wants to stay in touch with you on a weekly basis, pending your availability. Set up a standing meeting and/or call with your consultant to discuss what was accomplished since the previous call. This meeting also serves as an opportunity for you to update the consultant on any pertinent events that happened since your last meeting together, such as discussions with investors, vendors, and so forth, that could affect elements of the strategic plan. Ask your consultant to provide a written update on a weekly basis to serve as a paper trail, which will make it easier for you to communicate progress to your board of directors and/or investors.

Tip Have the turnaround consultant provide you with weekly updates, in writing, on the progress of the turnaround. The reports will serve as a record of actions taken and will make it easier for you to keep board members and investors apprised.

At some point, it makes sense to have your consultant present her interim findings to the board of directors. The more the board members are aware of the progress being made, the better it is for everyone involved. They need to know that hiring the consultant was a good investment. Periodic meetings throughout the initial phases of the engagement can go a long way toward getting buy-in from the board. Having the consultant talk to the board of directors and/or investors directly can alleviate a tremendous amount of pressure from the CEO. The consultant is less emotionally engaged, but is experienced at dealing with board members and thus able to handle any difficult questions thrown at her.

Don't Let Your Managers Shoot the Messenger

If you and your board of directors do your homework, you will have engaged a consultant that is going to tell you what she thinks you *need* to hear, not what she thinks you *want* to hear. This is the biggest difference between a consultant that is just trying to get as many billable hours out of you as possible and a consultant that takes pride in providing value to your company. A consultant that is committed to helping you fix your company's problems is not always going to agree with you. The more she gets to know your company, your products, your customers, your staff, and the market forces at play, the more opinionated she is going to become regarding the internal changes that need to occur for your company to prosper. This should be viewed as a good thing for your company.

Tip The consultant you engage should eventually start offering strong opinions on what needs to change in your company. If she doesn't, you may have hired the wrong consultant.

At some point during the turnaround process, the easy recommendations are going to have been made and accepted, and the more difficult issues are going to have to be faced. One of the first major challenges will be related to members of your management team. A consultant will inevitably come to the conclusion that one or more of your managers is not in the right position, and she will have solid evidence to back up her claim. If you are lucky, this recommendation will be accepted immediately by you and the respective manager, and a good solution will be found and agreed to by all.

However, there may be some pushback from that manager. Given your company's current predicament, you have a responsibility to do whatever will give your company the best chance to survive and, eventually, thrive. In the long run, these managers may come to realize they are better off having accepted their changed role. In the short term, however, they may be resistant to change. If you agree on the rationale for the change, you need to support the consultant's recommendation, but note that you risk losing your manager. If you cannot find a viable compromise, let the manager decide either to act on the recommendation or to resign. If he comes around, he will have set an example of doing what is best for the team. If he does end up resigning, the company will be better off in the long run; anyone resistant to change will not be helpful to the company moving forward.

In some cases, the manager might try to fight the recommendation by taking the low road and conducting a "character assassination" on the consultant. A professional turnaround consultant is used to this behavior and does not take it personally. However, it is critical that you understand that, if you do nothing about this negative situation, it will hurt the chances of your company achieving its turnaround and will be detrimental to employee morale. If the manager persists in his attacks, you have no choice but to let him go as soon as possible, as an example to your team that you are serious about doing what it takes to turn the company around.

And Don't Shoot the Messenger Yourself

One of the biggest challenges you face in turning your business around is accepting the recommendations your consultant makes regarding where your time is best spent based on the consultant's perception of the company's needs and your strengths. It is ironic that one of the first things I am told by CEOs when I conduct my initial interviews is how tired they are because they are spread too thin. I usually get confirmation on this point as well as a candid assessment of their strengths and weakness from their managers during the confidential interviews I conduct. There is usually consensus among management regarding where the CEO's time is best spent and which areas of the business the CEO should delegate to someone who is better qualified. Often I make recommendations about where the CEO should spend more of his time and where he should give up control, all hell breaks loose. Not surprisingly, I'm the bad guy in the eyes of the CEO—and suddenly I'm the punching bag for all his pent-up frustrations. In some instances, a CEO simply has a problem delegating, or has a martyr complex, which I believe is a sign of burnout or an inflated ego. I could play a different game and work around the CEO and not deal with the elephant in the room. However, if I did, I would lose my self-respect and compromise my professional integrity. I could go behind the CEO's back and speak directly to the board of directors. However, this is deceptive and counterproductive. What is so ironic is that my recommendations are what they are—recommendations. They are never binding. They are made, however, with the best interest of the company in mind, regardless of how difficult it may be for management to accept them.

The point in sharing this information with you is because you may be prone to the same negative reaction. It may be that you challenge any recommendation, but especially one so bold as to alter your daily responsibilities. However, if the recommendations are based on prudent assessments by a professional and are supported by your managers, you have a responsibility not only to yourself, but also to your employees and your shareholders to step up to the plate and show real leadership. Do what is necessary to protect the future of your company.

The alternative—ignoring the advice of and lambasting the consultant—should not be an option. Do so usually ends up being a death sentence for your company. It is important to point out that if you seek funding from venture capitalists, many will come in and force a change of your role as part of their terms and conditions for investing their capital. Do not take your consultant's recommendations personally. Keep your pushback of her recommendations on a professional level, rather than impugn the very person who may be one of the few actually trying to get you out of the hole you're in.

Do Not Revert to Bad Habits After the Consultant Leaves

At some point, you and your consultant will agree that she has completed her contractual obligations and has nothing more to contribute to your company's turnaround. Conduct an exit interview with your consultant to garner any last bit of candid insight that could benefit your company. Bring the consultant back periodically for a reality check or to assist with a specific challenge you are having difficulty overcoming.

The danger you and your management team may face after your turnaround consultant has left the scene is to fall back into your old bad habits. You may even be tempted to undo whatever initiatives the consultant convinced you and your board of directors to undertake. If you find yourself doing this without any data to support your actions, you will have just wasted a lot of time and money, and probably are putting the final nail in your company's coffin. Many of your investors who want to see you succeed and who were supportive of the consultant's recommendations will lose faith in you and your abilities to turn the company around. They will view their investment as a loss, and will move on to other deals that show a better chance of success. I know what I have written may sound harsh; however, it is better you hear it from me now, rather than later from angry investors after your firm ends up bankrupt or shut down.

Tip Don't fall back into your bad habits, or dismantle new initiatives, after the consultant leaves. Keep the momentum of change going. It may be your last chance to succeed.

Use the Strategic Plan as Your Compass

When you are in a moment of high stress and contemplating undoing something that the consultant had advised you against, go back and look at the strategy documents that the consultant and your team put together. Although this document, like most, has a limited shelf life, it was developed with input from all members of your team, including yourself. It should serve as your compass and road map to turn your company around. Chances are pretty slim that market trends would change so radically, in such a short period of time, to make obsolete the assumptions and the strategic and tactical recommendations made in the document. If the market *has* shifted, update the document and share the new reality with your management team to garner their buy-in. Rehire your consultant if necessary.

Summary

Hiring and managing effectively an experienced turnaround consultant is a big step in your quest to turn your company around. Have a clear set of expectations regarding what you hope the consultant will achieve. Selecting the most appropriate consultant based on his or her experience, the proposal submitted, references, and your personal comfort level in being able to work with him or her.

After the consultant is engaged, introduce him or her to your management team and to key staff throughout the company. It is important that you and the consultant stay in regular contact and exchange pertinent information. In addition, have your consultant submit a weekly progress report.

Do not allow your managers to sabotage the consultant's efforts. This is equally true for yourself if the consultant recommends a partial role change for you that you don't agree with. Do not take recommendations as personal affronts; do not get personal when pushing back on a recommendation.

Lastly, when the consultant leaves, don't revert to bad habits. If you are tempted to do this, remember to use your strategic plan as your compass to help you stay on course.

CHAPTER

12

How to Manage Yourself and Your Staff Better

Never Stop Believing in Yourself or Your Team

This chapter's objective is to help you put the entire book into context, in a large part, by helping you manage yourself and your staff better. Everything up to this point is relatively doable. If there is still a market need for your products and/or services, it is practically impossible not to make significant performance improvements by implementing as many of the recommendations made in this book as you can. Doing so will affect your company's cash flow positively, thereby buying you more time to turn your company in the direction you want to lead it.

I have made my recommendations in this book based on my experiences dealing directly with all the issues covered. I am confident that if I had read a book like this when I was facing my own business challenges, I would certainly have worked through them faster and more effectively. This is not to say that it would have guaranteed my companies would ultimately achieve the goals I set out for them; however, it certainly would have allowed me to fight the fight more effectively. This is one of the reasons why I was motivated to write this book. I take great pride and satisfaction in being able to help others when I am in a position to do so.

It is important to note that I come from the School of Tough Love. I tell all my clients, before they accept and sign my consulting proposals, that part of the value I offer is telling them what *I* think they need to hear and not what *they* want to hear. Their employees are probably already telling them what they want to hear, in part for fear of losing favor or even their job if they tell their boss what they really think. Not only is this type of culture not conducive to solving problems, but also it can exacerbate problems. Simply stated, an environment that does not allow constructive criticism is not a learning environment. If a firm is not learning, it is stagnating. Your firm can no longer afford to be stagnant.

The culture of learning is defined, in a large part, by the top executive. Based on my own entrepreneurial experience and consulting for dozens of companies during the past 20 years, a critical factor that is often overlooked for any organization to be successful is the individual performance of its top executive. Therefore, it is imperative that, as you develop a strategic plan for your company, you also develop a plan for how you are going to work smarter and more effectively. This chapter's goal is to help you start that process.

Note You need to be at the top of your game to engineer a turnaround. All eyes are on you and your employees will take your lead.

Take Responsibility for Your Actions: Stop Blaming Others

As mentioned in earlier chapters, culture trumps strategy. You, as the leader of your company, set the tone of your firm's culture far more than you may be aware. Therefore, having a positive attitude is absolutely essential to leading the process of turning your company around. And you cannot possibly be emanating a positive attitude if you are going around the company blaming others—consciously or unconsciously—for all your company's problems.

Yes, the 2008 recession hurt your business, as it did tens of thousands of other businesses. However, lots of companies have made their necessary strategic and operational changes and are back on offense. Sure, we all have listened to so-called experts and seasoned senior managers that talked the talk, but didn't walk the walk—and they made matters worse for the company. However, those people did not make any decisions without your approval. Most likely, they have not been working for you for several months or years now. Accept that mistakes have been made, learn from them, and move on.

It is also probably true that some of your better managers have left your firm or were laid off because of budget cuts. Thus, it goes without saying that less qualified and even unqualified employees were elevated to their current roles without having the breadth and depth of experience necessary to do their jobs successfully. I am sure the list of your challenges goes on and on. However, one of the most important points I have made throughout this book is that you must accept and even embrace the fact that you are in a new game. Harping on past mistakes, regardless of who is responsible for them, or reminiscing about the glory days of your company is not going to help you and your team get in the right frame of mind to undertake what is a difficult task for the most talented of teams in the best of circumstances.

It is important that you let your managers and staff know there will be no more finger pointing. Now is the time to fix the problems at hand. Encourage your staff to move on and to adopt a positive attitude to focus on the new horizon.

Focus on Working Smarter, Not Harder

In our American business culture, there are very few entrepreneurs and/or successful executives that do not bust their ass every day, every week, and every month of every year. Yet, it is wise for you to take a full day off every week just to let your mind take a break from all the stress with which you are dealing. Stress clearly has an impact on your physical well-being, which then affects your mental well-being; the two are interconnected. Often, those who have mental, physical, and spiritual balance in their lives are more productive and enjoy a better quality of life than those who do not take care of their total well-being.

When I was a just out of college, I lived at home for a year to help my dad close down a 50-year-old retail business. It was a very sad and stressful period in my parents' lives. One of the things my mom encouraged me to take away from the experience was to never skimp on accountants, doctors, and lawyers. It was probably the best advice she ever gave me and it has been a tremendous help to me, especially in difficult times. Part of working smarter is being willing to seek the advice and counsel of outside professionals when the situation calls for them. Let's review a few experts with whom you should consider speaking.

Tip Don't try to do fix the company all by yourself. Hire the services of those who can do a task better than you, which frees you up to do what you do best.

Accountant

If you have not already done so, meet with your accountant to update him or her on the situation your company is facing and get advice on how to best navigate through these difficult times based on his or her expertise. Your accountant may be able to recommend other experts to provide much-needed assistance, and they may even reduce their fees, until your company gets back on track, because they don't want to lose you as a client.

Lawyer

I also recommend that you meet with your corporate as well as a personal attorney. Again, they should be apprised of the situation with the aim of getting advice on how best to navigate through these difficult times based on their expertise. They, too, may be able to recommend other experts to provide much-needed assistance at a reduced fee until your firm is on more solid ground.

Spiritual Leader

Regardless of your faith, consider reaching out to your religious leader for spiritual guidance and comfort. Today, religious leaders deal with a myriad of social issues. Hence, your spiritual leader may be able to provide a very healthy perspective along with sound advice based on having talked with other people in similar situations. If you are not religious, perhaps yoga, meditation, or nonbusiness reading may provide you with some emotional relief and perspective. It is important to find a healthy outlet to help relieve you of the tremendous amount of stress with which you are dealing.

Doctors

If you have not already done so, get your annual physical. An unhealthy amount of stress long term is not good for your health. Even if you don't go into the details, let your doctor know that you are dealing with a tremendous amount of stress with your work. Depending on your age, he or she may recommend that you also take a stress test and/or undergo a heart scan or colonoscopy. I also recommend that you have a dental and vision checkup. A good bill of health will give you confidence in knowing that your body is healthy enough to get you through this stressful period in your life. Healthy test results will also comfort your family and friends in knowing that you are not literally killing yourself with work. It will also give confidence to your investors that the horse they bet on is healthy enough to continue to lead the company.

Diet

There is a plethora of evidence that a healthy diet enables people to function better. Eating too much unhealthy food along with drinking too much soda, coffee, and alcohol may take the edge off for a few minutes, but only adds to your stress later. Take small steps when changing your diet, so that the changes you make are sustainable. If this is new territory for you, consult a nutritionist. I had a nutritionist come to my home and go through my pantry and refrigerator to let me know what I should stop eating and what I should eat more of. Some nutritionists will even go to the grocery store with you to teach you how to shop for healthier foods. Your first step is to start immediately by drinking more water during the day. Eat more grilled fish and vegetables, and less red meat and fried foods. To satisfy an afternoon craving, snack on an apple, banana, or orange rather than chips and chocolate.

You can help your staff eat better by providing fruit in your company kitchen area. Consider not reordering sodas; replace them with bottled water instead. If you order food for a staff meeting, order only healthy foods, such as fruit, bagels, salads, and pasta, rather than pizza or donuts. These little changes will help your staff members start to take small but meaningful steps in improving their own diet.

Exercise

Even if you hate exercising, it is important that you force yourself to adopt a fitness routine several times a week. I appreciate the fact that you probably feel like you have no time to think, much less time to exercise. Find a friend or family member and start walking and/or going to an exercise class together. This way, you will feel like you're maximizing your time. I like to run and, for the past 20 years, I have running dates with business associates and friends. In many instances, having someone to confide in, regardless of the topic, was much more beneficial to my health that day than the actual run. When I don't have time to run, I take the stairs in a building, rather than the elevator. There have been times that I have been so stressed out with work that I didn't want to face the day. However, once I start exercising and those endorphins kick in, my attitude changes completely, and I feel much more ready to tackle the challenges of the day. I also know from personal experience that when I am on a regular exercise routine, I sleep better. Whatever exercise you choose to do, it should be fun; otherwise, you won't do it and the task just becomes one more impossible challenge on your list. Find something you like to do as soon as possible and start doing it on a regular basis, preferably with someone else.

Tip The payoffs of a regular exercise routine are enormous. You may think you don't have time to exercise, but in reality you don't have time not to. Besides a physically fit body, you will achieve better stamina, reduced stress, and greater clarity about solutions to problems, in addition to benefitting from a break from the workday and its barrage of challenges.

Encourage your staff to start exercising as well. When you have a staff meeting, ask your team what type of exercise they prefer. Share with your staff the changes you are making. Let them know that you are starting an exercise routine; tell them how it makes you feel. Practice what you preach and begin a staff meeting with a one-minute breathing or stretching exercise.

Sleep

Most Americans do not get enough sleep, which clearly affects their ability to function at their optimum level. Chances are that you might fit into this category. Ironically, many people who are stressed out have a hard time sleeping so they watch TV or surf the Web into the wee hours of the night. Determine the optimum amount of sleep you need (usually six to eight hours for adults) and force yourself to start going to bed earlier until you are confident you are getting enough sleep. If you feel good when you wake up in the morning, you are probably getting enough sleep. When I hit my mid 40s, I even started to take short naps on weekends. It helps me decompress a bit more.

All these recommendations have to be taken into the context of your own personal situation. You know how you function at your optimal level. I am merely trying to help you dedicate some time and energy into thinking about how you can function better, given all the issues you are facing. None of the recommendations in this chapter are going to solve your business challenges; however, collectively they may be able to help you relieve some stress, gain some perspective, and increase your energy level—all of which helps you function more effectively.

Family

No business is worth the price of your relationship with your spouse, significant other, or kids. Make time for the people who care about you the most and who are dependent on you for more than just a paycheck. Try not to talk about your business all the time when you are with your family and friends. Having grown up in a family business, I know this is easier said than done, but focus on how they are doing and what they want to talk about. Doing so gives you a much-needed break from your work and comforts your loved ones, who are also probably feeling stressed about your work situation or neglected by it.

Encourage your team members who work too much to stay away from the office at least one day during the weekend to clear their minds and spend quality time with their loved ones. Allow your to team to bring their immediate family and/or significant others when you have an employee outing.

Tip Don't talk about business all the time.

LEARN FROM PAST MANAGEMENT MISTAKES

Obviously, this entire book is about learning from past mistakes. However, I want you to focus more on learning from your past mistakes as they relate to your management style, rather than the specific decisions that were made. Collectively, your employees, consultants, and advisors should produce more output toward the company's success than you. Your role as CEO is to lead the effort, not to have everyone watch you do all the heavy lifting. Therefore, figure out ways in which you can become a better leader—improve your listening skills, be a better planner, be more consistent with the way you treat all your employees, and become better at holding yourself and your team more accountable for their performance or lack thereof. You may be the CEO, but you need to hold yourself to the same standards you hold your employees.

Set Expectations

Clearly, having an updated strategic plan is an important start in setting expectations for all your staff. However, your plan has a much better chance of succeeding if your team understands the plan and buys into it by knowing their role and responsibilities in relation to the plan. Let's review each of these points.

Understanding the Plan

After you, members of your team, and/or your consultant finish your strategic plan, it is important you determine

- Who in your company needs to know which aspects of the plan
- The best way to communicate the relevant portions to appropriate staff members
- The most appropriate time to communicate with each group of employees on your team

Acquiring this information should not be too difficult. Your senior managers need to know the entire plan, including its financial aspects. This knowledge will allow them to understand more completely the new financial goals toward with they are managing. Your rank-and-file staff need to know and understand the big picture, and how their department and they themselves fit into it.

The firm's top managers should review the various elements of the plan with your staff, which shows that the plan is supported by top leadership. This strategy also allows for any and all questions to be answered without the input of middle managers, who may or may not know the answers.

Buying into the Plan

It is critical that every level of management and staff buy into the plan if it is to have any chance of succeeding. First and foremost, it is critical that you and your executive team buy into the plan. If you don't buy into a plan that either your management team or outside consultant has developed, you need to bridge the gap immediately! There is no time to waste. Ask yourself: Which specific parts of the plan don't I like and why? What is a better alternative for the company to pursue and why? It is critical that you be as specific and constructive as possible. Although an ideal plan has input from every level of employee, the implementation of the plan must be driven by top leadership. If you, as CEO and/or founder of the company, don't buy into the plan, you will inadvertently undermine it. I speak from experience as one who develops strategic plans for companies. If your board authorizes a consultant to develop a plan it likes and you don't buy into it, you run the risk of being out of favor with your board, which could lead to your removal from your current position. Worse, the plan most likely won't work if you're not behind it. Therefore, it is imperative that you reach consensus. Compromise should not be seen as a weakness, but rather as a sign of commitment to what's best for the company's success.

If you are driving the plan and some of your fellow leaders are not buying into it, find out why immediately. If they do not understand your plan, take the time to explain it in depth. This is important, because they have to sell the plan to their rank-and-file staff. If they have valid concerns, address the concerns in a manner that shows them that you hear them and respect their input. This tactic helps to ensure their buy-in. It is critical that positive energy about the plan permeate the entire organization. You may have a manager or two who do not buy into the plan—even after you have explained it in more depth and have addressed all the concerns they expressed. If this is the case, you must ask yourself whether these managers should still be part of your team. It may be they no longer share your new vision for company and it is time for them to move on. If this is the case, the sooner this transition happens, the better it will be for them and for your company.

Your rank-and-file staff will most likely buy into the plan if it makes sense to them. This presentation may take some selling, and in more than one discussion. I am often engaged by management to develop a strategic plan and then present elements of it to the rank-and-file staff. Some staff members understand and embrace the new plan immediately, primarily because some of the changes were actually derived from my original interviews with them. Other staff members need more time, as well as some tangible results from the new plan, before they buy into it completely. They know things have to change, but they are skeptical that real change is going to occur. Another group may just happy to have a job and will go with the flow. A fourth group may have been taking advantage of the chaos the firm has been experiencing and will be somewhat resistant to change because it will require them to be more accountable. These folks may decide to resign or may be the first group of staff members to be terminated. Ultimately, the success of the new strategic plan in large part is dependent on your rank-and-file employees. Therefore, it is important that management is ensuring that employees' roles and responsibilities are in line with the plan on a weekly basis. Any gaps in what staff do on a daily basis related to the goals of the plan must be bridged immediately to ensure that the plan is being implemented successfully.

Leverage Your Strengths; Mitigate Your Weaknesses

If you are the founder of your company or a hired CEO, you have some amazing talents. The key is for you to leverage these talents as much as possible. The first step in doing this is to identify these strengths and to estimate how much of your time is actually spent on leveraging them. Given the challenges your company is facing, there is most likely a high probability that you are stretched too thin and thus not able to leverage what you do best. Find a way to change this situation as soon as possible. If you are not sure where your time should be best spent, ask your managers, your and your board of directors for their thoughts on this matter.

When I am engaged by a company to help with strategic planning, one of the first things I do is conduct confidential interviews with all managers and key personnel. During these meetings I ask the interviewees what they think their CEO does best and what responsibilities they think the CEO should give up. The challenge that many CEOs, and especially founders, face is to let go of responsibilities for which they are not well suited and focus more time and energy in the areas in which they excel. The ones who cannot delegate are either too emotionally engaged or are control freaks. If the previous sentence describes you, you may be one of the biggest impediments to turning your company around. This is why so many venture capitalists who invest in early-phase businesses and/or distressed businesses either remove the founder and/or CEO and replace him or her with their own hire, or change the role of the CEO/founder to maximize his or her strengths.

In all fairness to your current predicament, you and/or some of your managers may be in a position in which you have been forced to take on one or more roles that you would be happy to pass on to others who are more qualified—if your company could afford to hire them. If this is the case, include in your strategic plan how you plan to let go of these other roles and budget for the funding to hire these individuals.

Note Sometimes, you are the biggest impediment to your company's turnaround. Take a long, hard look at your role, personality, skills, and other attributes you bring to the job. Be honest with yourself. If you're not a net positive to the firm, you need to do what it takes to be more valuable to the firm or consider taking on a more focused role and bring in a new CEO to better leverage your skills.

Get Your Staff to Work Smarter

Many of the CEOs who hire me to help develop a strategic plan are burned out emotionally and physically, which may very well be the case with you. In most instances, I find it amazing these CEOs are still functioning, given what they have been through. In almost all instances, tenacity is certainly one of their off-the-chart strengths, which is why I started this chapter with a focus on getting you to work smarter and not harder. Part of your working smarter is to help your management and staff do the same. Sure, some of your staff could probably work harder, but this probably isn't why your company got into its current predicament. It is a much safer bet to assume that all your staff can work *smarter*.

After doing some self-assessment on how *you* can work smarter, spend more time focusing on how to get management and staff to work smarter. This shift must be a big part of the cultural change that must occur in your company if you are indeed going to turn it around. If you are running on fumes, there is a good probability that most of your loyal managers and rank-and-file staff are as well. If you are really good at some things and doing other things that are not good for the company's success, chances are that your management and staff have similar patterns.

It is your role to help break these patterns via your strategic plan and subsequent coaching and training to help your team work smarter. For example, there is no reason, in the proper context, that you cannot encourage your employees to take better care of their emotional and physical health by creating a wellness plan for them. The plan does not have to be complex or costly. There are plenty of online resources available to guide you in developing a wellness plan, as well as numerous consultants. If you have a payroll provider and/or offer health insurance to your employees, ask your representatives at these companies what resources they can provide to help create a wellness plan.

Tip Creating a wellness plan for your employees and leading by example are potent methods to help turn a company around. Exercise and other healthy changes will help the company break bad habits in other areas.

Protect Your Integrity; Don't Cut Corners

The last and most important piece of advice I can offer is for you to protect your integrity at all cost. My dad, who had more than his fair share of business challenges running a retail/wholesale business, always used to tell me and my siblings that, at the end of the day, all you have is your reputation. I understand all too well that we live in an era in which unethical business behavior almost seems to be the norm. Throughout the entire process of developing a plan to turn your company around, be ethical and honest. Tell the truth. Honor your commitments. If you cannot, then let the other parties know you can't and try to negotiate a settlement. If they won't budge, let the bankruptcy courts take over. Regardless of how bleak your situation appears, do not do anything illegal that could put your future into serious jeopardy or ask your staff to do something illegal on your behalf. You could not only end up losing your company, you could end up drowning in lawsuits—or sitting in jail.

Integrity should be part of your company culture. Instill it throughout your organization by example, by how you conduct yourself. Tell your managers that you expect them to act ethically and within the law at all times, with no exceptions! Then, communicate this to your rank-and-file staff.

I know it must feel like your world will come to an end if your company does not survive. And you certainly didn't buy this book for advice on what to do if your company does not make it. I have been there more than once. I am well aware of that terrible, horrifying feeling when you stare defeat in the face and realize that people's jobs are dependent on you. However, having been there, I also know that, regardless of the outcome, this phase of your life will pass and life goes on.

Summary

As the leader of your company, it is critical that you project a positive attitude not only for yourself but also for your staff. You cannot be optimistic if you are still playing the blame game. Focus on working smarter, in part, by seeking advice from your attorney, accountant, doctor, lawyer, and spiritual leader. Take better care of your health by exercising, eating a healthy diet, getting a good night's sleep, and by spending more time with your family. Encourage your management and staff to work smarter as well, in part by helping them learn from past mistakes.

Make sure you and your management team thoroughly understand and endorse your strategic plan. Thereafter, all employees should be told of the plan and how their role and responsibilities tie in to it. To have the best chance of implementing your plan successfully, make sure that you leverage your strengths and mitigate your weaknesses. Then, apply this tactic to your entire staff. Most important, protect your integrity. Do not cut corners; never ask your staff to do something unethical or illegal. Your reputation is your most important asset. Last, never ever stop believing in yourself and in the other members of your team.

I hope this book provides some type of lifeline for your company's turnaround. Most important, I hope it reminds you that there is much for you and your staff to be proud of. Never, ever stop believing in yourself or your team. Good luck.

Sample Consulting Proposal

June 4, 2013

Mr. Jones, CEO
Newco Security
123 Main Street, Suite 456
Houston, TX 77025

Dear Mr. Jones,

ROI is pleased to present Newco Security with its proposal to provide advisory services to develop Newco Security's strategic operational plan to put it back on the path to revenue growth.

The planning effort is structured in two phases, with specific areas of focus as laid out in the attached proposal detail. During phase 1, ROI will conduct an internal and external assessment from which the strategic operational plan will be developed. On adoption of the plan, ROI, during phase 2, will assist in developing a strategy to help find investors to fund the next stage of growth for Newco Security and to help with the implementation of the strategic plan. ROI agrees to complete the effort required to conduct phase 1 within a four- to six-week period, commencing on signing the attached agreement, accompanied by the first installment of agreed-on fees.

ROI is ready to begin work on phase I immediately and looks forwards to working with Newco Security's management to improve and increase its revenues.

Sincerely,

Jonathan Lack, Principal
ROI Ventures, LLC

Background

Newco Security has reached a stall point in its market growth such that it is seeking to raise $10 million to $15 million. To do so, it needs an interim infusion of $500k to $750k to be able to meet is current payable obligations to ensure ongoing production, secure its operational base, and achieve higher gross profit margins. It also needs to develop and put into operation a disciplined strategic operational plan to identify critical growth opportunities in the security market and resume a growth path. This operational plan will be based on a clearly articulated internal and market audit so that the firm's direction becomes less susceptible to personality or relationship-based distractions. On review of the plan by management and subsequent adoption, Newco Security will be able to provide a coherent rationale and a disciplined growth strategy to investors during the larger investment round of phase 2.

Activities for Phase I

ROI is prepared to commit its principal to a full-out "sprint" for four to six weeks to support the following activities.

Internal Operational Assessment/Audit

ROI will execute confidential interviews with key staff members (including the chief executive officer and key board members) to assess internal perspectives on the following nonexclusive list of issues: the company's strengths and weaknesses, areas for corporate improvement, perceptions on where key staff members think the company can improve, perception of how decisions are made, and overall employee morale. In conjunction with the interview effort, ROI will undertake a review of all major internal documents, including existing strategic plans, financials, and marketing and sales plans. ROI expects this activity to require an onsite visit for several days.

External Market Assessment

Complementing the internal assessment effort, ROI will undertake three interrelated external assessment efforts for the purposes of benchmarking Newco Security's comparative market position and potential obstacles to growth targets. The first effort will focus on the market landscape, including security market trends subdivided and cross-analyzed by segments (subject to data availability), including financial, demographic, and psychographic metrics. The second effort will focus on an assessment of competitor strategies and activities across these same segments, with one purpose being to build a segmented market model that can be used to assess unexploited market niches that Newco Security could develop with comparative advantage. The third and final effort will be focused on assessing what go-to market strategies were executed by companies with analogous market-changing innovations, with the goal being to determine what unique (or better, common) strategies Newco Security could replicate for increasing market penetration of its security technology.

Development of the Strategic Plan

After conducting the first two sets of activities, ROI will develop the first draft of a strategic plan that will provide, at a minimum, ROI's assessment of Newco Security's market position; where Newco Security needs to position itself realistically to achieve revenue growth that provides a return to investors; a gap assessment that highlights the critical delta elements between the two; a SWOT (Strengths, Weaknesses, Opportunities, and Threats) analysis that identifies market and internal obstacles to achieving growth, and that indicates which comparative advantages and disadvantages Newco Security has in overcoming the identified gaps; and, last, the strategic plan itself, which represents the courses of action management is advised to undertake to resume an expansion of company revenues. ROI expects this activity will entail an effort spanning the entire four- to six-week period indicated earlier.

Summary Table of Deliverables and Fees for Phase I

The following is a summary table of all key activities and deliverables that ROI anticipates providing to Newco Security.

Task	Deliverable	Fee
Internal operational assessment/audit	Operational assessment Timeframe: 1–1.5 weeks	A total of $40,000 in consulting fees, paid in two equal installments, plus additional expenses such as travel, copying, and so forth billed at cost
External market assessment	Market segmentation analysis Competitor strategy assessment Analogous innovator strategy assessment Timeframe: 2–2.5 weeks	
Development of the strategic plan	Strategic plan draft 1 Timeframe: 1–2 weeks	

Activities for Phase 2

The importance of instituting strategic planning into Newco Security's modus operandi is not only essential for operational success, but also to acquire additional funding. It is important that your investors know what your short-term and long-term funding needs are to keep the business solvent and to thrive. The strategic plan will provide Newco Security's management team a more disciplined approach to turning the company around, and it will signal to investors that management will avoid false paths chosen on an ad hoc basis.

Consequently, on adoption of the strategic plan, ROI is prepared to assist in helping to develop a strategy to find investors to fund the next stage of growth for Newco Security. This includes but is not limited to assisting in preparing a fund-raising deck and reviewing offering documents, in addition to other activities as arranged. ROI is also prepared to help with the implementation of the strategic plan.

Summary Table of Deliverables and Fees for Phase 2

A separate proposal and summary table for phase 2 will be submitted based on a needs assessment provided by Mr. Jones after phase 1 is completed.

Terms and Fees

ROI prides itself on devoting attention to its clients to meet their needs. ROI shall apply the attention and energies of ITS principal indicated to the business as required by this proposal. ROI shall not, during the term of this engagement, be precluded from engaging in any other business activity with other ROI clients.

Phase 1 activity fees are to be paid as follows:

- **$40,000 total, paid in two installments:** The first installment is due on commencement of work as agreed on between Jonathan Lack and Mr. Jones. The second installment will be due on delivery of the first draft of the strategic plan.
- **Expenses billed at cost**: Typically, ROI clients can expect expenses to total less than 5% of the total project budget when travel is involved; expenses range from 1% to 2% when travel is local. All expenses relating to the project will be invoiced at the end of each month and must be paid by the 15th of the following month.

In conclusion, I welcome the opportunity to review any section of this proposal with you for clarification. Feel free to add or tweak any section you deem necessary. It is critical that you are a 100% comfortable with the project scope before we undertake any of the associated activities.

I look forward to working with you

Jonathan Lack, Principal
ROI Ventures, LLC

Agreed to and Accepted By:

Signature __________________________ Date ______________

Name and Title __________________________

Biography

Jonathan H. Lack, Project Manager. Jonathan H. Lack is principal of ROI Ventures. He has more than 20 years' post-MBA experience in management and strategic planning, focusing primarily on consumer product, manufacturing, and services companies. He has worked with and for companies of all sizes—startups, midsize, and *Fortune* 500—in a variety of industries, including finance, food and beverage, information services, health care, Internet, manufacturing, and telecom. Lack served as Director of Alternative Investments for Galapagos Partners, LP, a Multi-Family Office, in which he currently advises on special projects. Lack was also a member of the founding executive management of Houston–based CompuBank, NA, the first Internet bank to receive a charter from the Office of the Comptroller of the Currency. In that role, he helped raise $36 million in institutional funding from Goldman Sachs, SoftBank, General Electric, and Marsh & McLennan. As chief strategist and marketing officer for CompuBank he built a staff and led a program that resulted in one of the industry's fastest growth rates. In addition, his group developed brand recognition and customer confidence programs that earned CompuBank the number one ranking in online banking by the *Wall Street Journal's SmartMoney* magazine. In May 2001, CompuBank's accounts and deposits were sold to NetBank, a public Internet bank based in the United States. Lack holds an MBA from the University of Pennsylvania's Wharton School of Business, a master's degree in International Relations from Johns Hopkins University's School for Advanced International Studies, and a bachelor's degree in Middle East Studies from the University of California at Berkeley.

I

Index

C

D

E

F, G, H

I, J, K

L

M, N, O

P, Q

U

W, X, Y, Z

CPSIA information can be obtained
at www.ICGtesting.com
Printed in the USA
LVHW030828041221
705271LV00001B/3